Configurations

Clarence Major

Configurations

NEW AND SELECTED POEMS 1958–1998

CLARENCE MAJOR

COPPER CANYON PRESS

Printed in the United States of America.

The publication of this book was supported by grants from the Lannan Foundation, the National Endowment for the Arts, and the Washington State Arts Commission. Additional support was received from Elliott Bay Book Company, Cynthia Hartwig, and the many members who joined the Friends of Copper Canyon Press campaign. Copper Canyon Press is in residence with Centrum at Fort Worden State Park.

LIBRARY OF CONGRESS CATALOGING-IN-PUBLICATION DATA
Major, Clarence.
Configurations: new and selected poems, 1958–1998 / Clarence Major.
    p. cm.
ISBN 1-55659-090-3
1. Afro-Americans – Poetry. 1. Title.
PS3563.A39 C59 1998
811'.54 – DDC21   98-40085
                                  CIP

9 8 7 6 5 4 3 2 FIRST EDITION

COPPER CANYON PRESS
Post Office Box 271
Port Townsend, Washington 98368

CONTENTS

From

Some Observations of a Stranger at
Zuni in the Latter Part of the Century *1989*

New and Previously Uncollected Poems *1958–1998*

Configurations

Clarence Major

From

SWALLOW THE LAKE

1970

SWALLOW THE LAKE

gave me things I
could not use.   Then.   Now.
Rain night bursting upon and into –
I shine up-down into Lake Michigan

like the glow from the lights of the Loop.
       Walks. Deaths. Births. Streets.
Things I could not give back –
       or use. Gave me loneliness.
Feelings I could not put into words
       into people. Blank monkeys of the hierarchy!
More deaths! Stupidity and death
turning them on, timing them
       to the beat of my droopy heart,
to my Middle Passage blues
to my self-corroding hate –

In my release, I come to become
       neon iron eyes stainless lungs
blood zinc-gripped steel
I come up abstract –
not able to take their bricks.
       Their tar. Their flesh. Their plastic.
I ran – stung.
Loop fumes hung in my smoky lungs.

Duped, left with ideas I could not break
          or form,
I crawled through the game.

Illusion illusion and you
          would swear before screaming –
these choked voices in me screaming.

Screaming with crawling thing in the blood,
          screaming the huge immune loneliness.
One becomes immune to the bricks
          to the feelings.
One becomes death.
One becomes each one and every person I become.
And I could not –
          I could not –
I could not whistle and walk in storms
along Lake Michigan's shore.
          Concrete walks. Concrete deaths.
I could not –
I could not swallow the lake.

KITCHEN CHAIR POEM #4

So they fought – not easy himself
to cope with. It was also around this time
that the boxer began to really see,
to ease up from the girl next door.
This girl was made unhappy
because her baby died – frail girl,
alone in her small room,
if I remember correctly.
How strange, the small baby
reaching toward anything motherlike.
How strange
her sticky candy fingers
twisted,
and sour milk all over her face.
She almost managed to live,
growing sticks for arms and legs
small and weak. Someone once walked her
in a neglected park and she crumbled.
Somebody walked her again
in the neglected park and she buckled.
One night she rolled over onto a radiator –
      her tiny ribs arms face grilling,
frying all night, while her mother, drunk and wet
with a fighter boxing in his sleep
      on her, with the TV still going.

KITCHEN CHAIR POEM #5

Truck driver, second-floor roomer.
Good for next month's rent?
A screaming silence fell down three flights
and hit the basement.
Couldn't last any longer –
      her getting by like.
The jealousy. These others
with husbands who still had teeth.
Every broad in the building screamed
down into her room – screaming on her
      to make it, to get her hat –
scrape the wind outside. The blowing December
slabs nailed her against herself,
      against her own desperation.
And they had no idea why
      she split without a fight.
All those strikes against her.
Like this dude said
      who'd just come out of prison,
Man I can't even afford to look
      with my eyes funny.

MY SEASONAL BODY

For that whole year I was in the weight of myself.
I was a hundred and fifty pounds of sadness

in a warm locality with sky and boats and sea.

I was solitary and lonely.

I was sixteen with holes in my head for eyes.
I was so so serious.

The weight of my young self was so heavy.
So heavy.

WAITING IN THE CHILDREN'S HOSPITAL

I reflect on my son's crying
while waiting in the children's hospital.
The desperate cry of one slipping away
into death – cold as ice with closed eyes,
      after poison.

Benches and benches of blood.

Joyce and I walked home in the rain
and around midnight I scribbled a letter to my sister,
      dying five minutes at a time:
You are the flower of confusion
coming up in the morning
and going tightly shut in the afternoon.
I look forward to your resurrection.

I get up at night and walk naked
in the open through wet weeds.
The moon is smiling and it has no teeth.
I am homeless, I am homeless.

I remember a trillion stars
in the Lexington night and all shadows –
mine and others ahead and behind, but
I cannot remember the touch

of a little girl's kiss.
Does she remember?

I walked to town with a blind man
        beside me singing and singing.
That was the summer of a trillion grasshoppers.
His woman back there in a shack
        beside the highway
with four grandbabies in a wooden bed.
She fanned summer flies
from the syrup on their lips.

But the blood is white this summer.

Roasted ears. The hog season and my uncle
        was a good shot.
The blood is red this summer
the blood is redder than redbirds
        this summer.

With the heart of a monk,
I stayed silent,
face flat to the earth
arms outstretched.
        And when I got up
I walked close to walls,
        moving with head low
and hands hidden.

THE DOLL BELIEVERS

This lifeless construction,
Yellow hair curled and twisted,
The forever motionless face of rubber,
The dark marked eyebrows,
The flexible pug nose,
Spongy red cheeks,
Camel's-hair eyebrows
Moving up and down.
Lifting her up, her eyes fly open,
They stare into space –
An unmoving blueness.
Those never winking, moving balls,
Controlled from the inside,
And that thick rubber body,
The imprint of a navel,
The undersized hands,
The thick soft knees,
The screwed-on head,
The air hole behind her neck,
All this in its lifelessness
Gives me a feeling
That children are amazing
To imagine such a thing alive.

NONE OF IT WAS

It was a long time
before I saw anything
like a seashore –
even the stockyards five blocks away.
But close and not a lie
was the pool of blood, animal blood.
I saw a long line of gulls early,
taste even now their cry.
But none of it is fumbled together,
        reflecting something
singular, nor was there
        in any of it a crisis.

From

PRIVATE LINE

1971

BILL'S

With defective thyroid glands,
I got up early –
no communication last night
with your ghost
but I dreamt of flint sickles.
Black, we know the cemetery.
Lot of land around here.
Boy down the hill arrested
in the process of his growth.
Don't know his name.
I'm here for only three days.
Locked myself out –
meant only to take in morning air.
But had to make do with the facts.
Necrosis in the tips of my fingers.
River down there and the yellow cat
followed me down across the tracks.
I sat on a rock alongside the water.
Dow Chemical across on the other side
with train tracks going there.
But I'm on this side looking way the other way
till Bill wakes and unlocks the door.

SAILING

Helping her with her knots,
I spread my sails in her storm,
put up the clamp,
put up my mast,
the clamp on it.
I put down her lines,
keeping my trust
in them – in the storm before dark.
We anchor and watch
our different ropes move
back toward our last turn
in the water. We time them
together against the breakers.

From

SYMPTOMS AND MADNESS

1971

DISMAL MOMENT PASSING

This is, this is –
this *has* to be here like this
because I am inconsolable.
Even summer coming
failed
to enlarge the green accuracy of Nature.
Real summer, we won't see till Mexico.
Anyway, I think of my mother when I think of Nature,
her beliefs – like sheets flapping on a back porch line.
Some people might still wash things
and hang them up to dry.
Children play on the sidewalk.
At least they are happy.
I sit in my own opaque opening,
but I promise
to be better tomorrow.

EIGHTEEN-DOLLAR TAXI TRIP TO
TIZAPAN AND BACK TO CHAPALA

A taxi driver
with a good life
who has four children,
a pregnant wife,
and who lives in
Guadalajara,
drives us –
(with his radio going
    cha cha cha
for these gringos)
on the road laid out
    and up and around
and down the side of
Lake Chapala to Tizapan.
Up ahead, three burros
move nervously
    out of the road
as we swish by.
I remember all we saw.
Gringos going into a storm
that soon ends
    to consider a room
(as it turns out)
filled with straw
upstairs over a bodega.

THE NERVE

The tracings around my edges?
Your black silk stockings.
My ripped sweater.
The hard knots of your outrage.
I hear peanuts spilling down an air shaft.

I touch the line of your thin brown lips.
The line of your eye, the other eye.

An eggy substance slushes through our nappy lashing.
This is all vanity in the mirror.
I trace a line through the memory of us.

We get enraptured in our own natures.
We've got a lot of nerve.
Everybody else is taking another approach.
We play with each other's toes on pink-green sheets.
Here we are in summer sunlight
with the nerve to touch our own mystery.

THE RAINY SEASON

Puerto Vallarta, Jalisco, Mexico
August 1968

You've never seen such a flat black ocean
a perfect straight line.
Now the sky is gray with no wrinkles.
Two inches thick from here
with soft-wash black telephone poles
      leaning against it,
crooked and old,
the thinnest things you ever saw.
Look at the corner of this brick wall.
(I have painted it several times.)
It changes color under the splatter of the rain.
Hear the thunder, see the lightning.
Out toward the *malecón* a huge black bird
      with wings as wide as a fan belt for a Ford
dives down into the deep ocean,
leaving a large clean spot open in the sky.
Now the edge of the sun floats
      as the mighty bird comes up,
and ducks again.
Across the street,
three white American station wagons
      parked against an orange brick wall
beside a white-faced hotel

with a black doorway.
This wall the trees the cars the traffic
        change before my eyes.
But now along the mountain range
        you see yellows that stay
put with the blues, touched gently
        by blue light.
Now a red truck very red in the rain
with halo-light around it
comes around the corner,
followed by a sleek brown nag,
ears down, pulling
        an old weatherworn wagon
as the cars plow through,
turning and slicing the water back
onto two women carrying washtubs,
        filled with wet clothes,
balanced on their heads.
A little bowlegged hombre
        beneath a large sombrero
and in a raincoat
drives his legs meanly up Hidalgo.

Now, the sun that must take
its time in going, comes out
        to finish.
The weather here is so strange.

Now, the ocean is gray
        and scorched the yellow of butter.
So are the river in the road
        and the green rocks
and the gold, the pink, lavender rocks.

MADMAN OF THE SOUTH SIDE

I met your husband in a bookshop.
His looks scared me shitless.

Yet I followed him everywhere.
Fear led to fascination.

He could measure the temperature
spectrum of stars,

outdrink Faulkner and Hemingway
together, fit perfect the shield

around a berth hawser
to keep out rats.

He claimed ancestors
among the Catawba and Shawnee.

To work a spell,
he would release their spirits

from a leather pouch.
But I guess he was right about me.

And I'm sorry you and I
ever touched each other.

FOOD FOR THOUGHT; OR, DEATH IS PHYSICAL

The cornstarch.
The potatoes.
The raisins.
The margarine.
The shredded oranges.
The rutabaga.
The egg white.
The ripe pineapple.
The lemon gelatin.
The tomato relish.
The lemon juice.
The Chinese cabbage.
The salt.
The pepper.

MOTHER JUNKIE

She has the shakes, thinks she's gonna die.
So thin turned sideways

in the mirror she disappears.
They keep telling her to cool it.

She's got fifteen cats and six litter boxes.
Stinks up the hallway.

Everybody in the building bitches
and she comes and goes hiding

behind dark glasses. Her night traffic
keeps me awake. She has fits.

She keeps telling them about her fits.
Her daughter keeps begging me

for a bike ride. Healthy girl
with a curious mind.

I take her on the handlebars, her first time
to the East River, five blocks away.

THE COTTON CLUB

Look at Duke!
He stays up and up.

Stays up in the music.
Up where the music reaches.

Up through the waves of the music.
His waves slicked back.

Duke's staying up all night
so long that time stays up with him.

But you can see the afternoon
in his eyes. Yellow sunlight going down.

And he sleeps late. Slow at home.
Remembering Jungle Nights.

Sailing on the wide wings
of a Blue Bird, sailing light.

And somebody's always saying
Hold it, Duke,

I wanna take your picture,
and they can't even see him.

From

THE SYNCOPATED CAKEWALK

1974

GIANT RED WOMAN

I have a delicious problem.
A huge woman is living in my office.
It's a quaint office in a purple cottage.
I don't know this woman
but her presence is an unfair delight.
When she speaks her voice
causes my body to vibrate.
Her woman-smell consumes me.
Her breasts push their way
out the two windows
toward the apple orchard.
She's too much – thighs hips arms hands
face feet neck ass, too much.
She continues to expand.
My desk is crushed,
the chairs are inaccessible,
the bookshelves are smashed,
the walls are cracking.
People who come to see me
say they can't see her,
that she's only in my head.
Yet they themselves
        are unable to enter.
This space is full –
        full of my own struggle to live.

I slide around the edges of her,
trying both to live with her
      and to escape.
Soon, movement will be impossible.
I can't enter her openings
      nor leave the office.
The pressure is liquid.
I wait here, against the wall.
This – this cannot go on.

WORDS INTO WORDS WON'T GO

There are no things rain is like.
Trees are like brick walls.
But there are no things the walls themselves are like.
I'm like you. The contents of a book are like margarine.
The hard green surface of my car is like a forest fire.
There are adventures in things I cannot pinpoint –
     like snow, a storm, or sleet.
The handyman who sweeps the leaves
     in the yard is not like himself.
German fiction is not like African fiction.
The umbrellas are like birds.
They fly in the rain.
The radio says we can expect snow.
The radio is not like itself.
There are no things the rain is like.
I am not like myself.
I am not myself.
I change but change is not itself.
There are no things change is like.

THE EXPANDED COMPOSITION

Let's see how we feel today.
She sits on a dirty bench in a green park.
She's sketching what's before her eyes –
    the silver fence, the wet sandbox,
the blue and purple buildings.
In the background the sky is clear.
One cloud in a cold and warm day already half-gone.
Country music coming from somewhere.
Memory of a red dirt road in Waycross, Georgia.

Can you hear my voice? These feelings belong to you!
Her pink hand moves in quick short strokes.
She wears dyed leather every day.
These feelings belong to your eyes.
Let's see how we feel again.
These feelings belong to your face
    and the memory of singing.
All songs are about being born
    and having to die.
All movement is part of the past.
The girl's presence is isolated.
Let's see how she feels now.
She's mistrusting and suspicious and angry.
Everything that once made sense
    to her now makes new sense.

I am deeply touched by her.
She leaves notes under my door while I sleep.
Memory of a broken sidewalk in Chicago.
She comes here every day to sketch.
The motion of her hand belongs to me.

READ THE SIGNS

I don't want to speak of your sky
     and my sea and their land
and our people – or of the cars
the roads the houses.
The sky is a long list of verbs.
The sea is its table of contents.
The landscape is something people move across.
Out of their cars,
     people themselves are like bushes near water.
They drink it through their roots.
The background tension you feel
     comes on because talking begins from fear.

These roads we use are actually dried-out rivers
that lead us into each other's lives.

THE WAY THE ROUNDNESS FEELS

A secret world turns in us.
Your fingers cruise the rotunda.
You handle your own canoe in water.
I hear your loud heart thumping under my hand.
Listen to my face. Stay with me.
I move around in the recurring circle
      that is my absence.
Feel the shape.
Feel how it must be in here
      where I sway.
Your neck and breasts are round.
So are our teacups.
They are necessarily shaped this way.
White, silver, and gold – the dark and light colors
      of our wholeness
are here in the shadows around us.
Your mouth, I know your lips.
Your hands, I know your fingers.
I feel you moving all through these words.
From inside of me you are speaking,
giving shape to my thoughts.

A LIFE STORY

I used to feel like fossil pollen,
and I spent my time roaming the Basque.
It was off-limits but it didn't matter.
My sense of self in the world itself
kept redreaming and replenishing itself.

I found almost anything
back then acceptable.
I even developed a theory
        to trace the Lost Tribes of Israel.
I was found everywhere anybody could see –
on the South Side whistling
        a *double* double-consciousness melody –
but being everywhere cost too much.

Now there's a chance I'll be deported,
just as I might have risen like a glacial area –
        slowly, from anger.
But I never thought twice about winning
because I always considered the self
        a little too dangerous in itself
to be messed with too much.
Funny thing how I never came across
        anybody else
with it worked out exactly like this.

FUNERAL

American Airlines to Chicago.
Mae is here grinning – the same cheeks
     I grew up touching.
I am her brother.
Carrying one of my heavy bags,
on the moving staircase,
she laughs and says:
"Man, what you got in this bag?"

My stepfather has died and
I am home for the funeral.
They have him propped up in the casket.
His face powdered,
he's neatly tucked in a suit
with his thick hands resting together
     on his bosom. We all share
this hysterical silence, a scream,
     then tears, then laughter.

Later, young and old from everywhere –
Kentucky Tennessee Virginia Georgia –
gather there in Mother's living room,
young folks sipping Coca-Cola,
     eating ice cream
while the old sip hard liquor.

And in the kitchen Mother,
        with her fried chicken and mashed potatoes
spread out all across the table, is talking with
the ladies – her sisters and aunts
        and cousins, people I don't know –
from Oklahoma, Arkansas, Alabama, you name it.

And an uncle on the couch is talking about Wichita Falls
last summer, about some fifty-year-old white woman
        who fell in love with him. *Daddy Daddy.*

Now morning again –
        and here we are at the gravesite
watching the body descend into the earth.
Pretending my eyes are closed,
I watch Mother.
What is there to say?
Her face does not know
        what expression to hold.

As we drive back,
I hold my ticket and Mae.

A GUY I KNOW ON 47TH AND COTTAGE

The day of the strong rap
does not build to a close.

I see it, the heavy plop, climb
from the mouths of twelve-year-olds

in backyards trying to be honey cats
like their fathers. Same

values – big cars giant hearts.
Laying a nickel on somebody

to impress the Lady. Grand
Theft Money. Moving up from lazy

bread to French muffins. Hawking foreign
chicks rather than mellow yella. In the future

I can just see him grown and slick
in a hog on a heavy map he thinks is the end,

the greatest. See him throwing a few dimes
to the Grape Society in the nearby alley.

He'll go to see his mama and sister about
once a month to lay a big buck on them,

knowing Mother's Day will not come
till the end of the month.

THE WOUNDED BULLFIGHTER

Blood on his torn glossy pants.
But the bull is down.
Brave, holding up the bull's ear,
he walks nearly falling.
The bright splash of people fumble in their cheering.
He makes a blunt move forward, out of the oval of shade.
But the bull gets up and comes from behind.

"Señor, the blood is dripping through the stretcher."
These simple facts close an afternoon.
They clear his pants and face of blood.

This part of his life is as blunt
as the front of a strange twilight.
But it is still today
and he is stretched out on an evening table.
His gold-and-blue suit no longer fits.
This part of his glory does not fit him well.
"And part of the lower stomach has been ripped away."
The doctor blew velvet smoke at the wife.
She sits waiting and waiting as for a bell.
"Internal bleeding in these cases is common.
The soft areas are in danger."
On the X ray, we see a slight bone chip.
For her, the goring hurts

way off somewhere unknown.
But her husband is resting,
and the bull, he is brave but dead.

COON SHOWMAN

Folks, this is of the Jonah Man.
He's under spotlights. Mister Nobody!
King of Bandanna Land!
A light-skinned colored man
in black paint. Glossy black
face under lights! Nobody sees
what's beneath the whipped grin,
beneath the years of memory
and vaudeville fame. And late hours
and poker-game skits,
so painful I see people moving
back from his dreams.
The entire aim, he says, is to be natural.
The point of the foot is to walk.
The mouth, to talk.
The eye, to see.
See Mister Nobody! The Jonah Man!
Hey! Jonah Man! whip it on them!
Hey! Coon Man! lookaheah, big shot!
Your paint hides nobody.
Nobody is beneath the grease,
the laughter; nobody rubbing elbows
with you in Matheney's Café 125th
and Seventh; while you are singing
and dancing one part of the self to pieces.

Yet there is another kind of death:
in the yellow shadows,
the face, at forty-seven, closes.
Always he wore his white gloves
to hide his yellow hands, now – dead,
they put them on him again. A symbol.
Yellow nigger! Yellow nigger!
How you gonna pass for black?
How you gonna pass for white?
King of Bandanna Land, Mister Nobody,
The Coon Man, The Jonah Man,
where you gonna hide your yellow?
Singing and dancing
each part of your passion to pieces!

SEXUAL CONDUCT

My pretty cousin, ten years old,
with her big strong hands,
stood me, six years old, in a washtub.
In alarm, when I turned man on her,
she called her mother,
"Ma! Juneboy acting mannish!"
breaking her own rhythm.
My very pretty cousin, she was high class,
even went to college,
but wouldn't let the soap move between my legs,
wouldn't trust the spirit of her own father.
In tears, she scrubbed my back but
refused to listen to the Indians, the Eskimos, the Gulf of
        Mexico
in her ears. And she's a girl who sings!
She screamed when I resembled her dreams.
Yet on Sunday she wore strings of magic
stretched like some wealthy shaman.
Now married, a son slid from her
like an egg from a bird.
He came out mannish!

FLOWERS FOR MY DATE

She dipped snuff.
Read comic books.
Smacked gum.
Told stupid jokes.
Fucked in hallways.
Played the dozens with her mama.
Now, here I come with a bunch
        of yellow flowers.

BEYOND IMPASSE

I climb the steps to my room.
Thinking of my bed, I unlock the door,
though I meant to do something else.
A Chinese girl, in purple, is by the window.
She tells me the pictures in her head.
I can barely see her.
An African is a man burning in her memory.
I look out the window.
I try to open the window. It's hot.
Outside, the landscape tries to escape
the trees planted in it. I try again.
The window won't open.
The African is now making love to the Chinese girl.
Is this a dream?
Is she dreaming this or am I?
Now, the Chinese girl says to me,
"Remove the African,
and I will show you how to open the window."

IN THE ARMPIT OF THE HILL

Dream of coffee beans rice codfish and bananas,
stacked under the chandelier tree.
The rain stopped; except in the mountains.
An old woman with pothooks for sale,
waves from the road.
The hens cackle. *In my sleep.*
I put the charcoal in the wicker basket. *As I sleep.*
You peel the skin back from the red fruit,
suck its juice till it is drained, then
return to our thatched covered hut.
Full. Happy. *A dream.*
Out in the wild grass, blight walks around
with an erection. I wonder how long this can go on.
Yesterday, we had cornmeal.
It tasted like oak bark.
The day before, the congo beans you stole broke
in the mouth like dead roots.
I do not complain for myself: but for the baby inside.
Down in Pétionville, they eat steaming hot fish.
My father died hungry, chewing his clay pipe.
Tomorrow, on the road, the Voodoo drums;
in the hills, the blue blossom of the breadfruit tree!
And, on our table, only the cactus plant.

BALLROOM DARK

With heavy eyelids I am still in love
with the high-ass girl
who dances fast and smooth
through heavy smoke.

And the music is still drunk and thick
with beer stains in it. Meat-packers
on the weekend are desperately dancing
with switchblades in back pockets.

Nothing changes. The darkness still moves
under the tables and along the walls,
where I hide my suffering
and my lust for the girl at the next table.

PUPA

Can she induce a dream?
Her dress is pink-green.
Her Turkish face is black.
She sits in the central part of a wheel.
In Arizona she is in a desert.
On the sand now she gets hot sunlight.
I swear I won't mean any of this when I wake.
An immobile insect, she is a secret.
She remains secretive as she stands
on her hands, then her knees.
As she waters the plants with care she touches them.
Between her fingers she holds, in upright wonder,
the unruly sunlight, kissing it with great devotion.
Can she survive my wakefulness? I kiss her,
I kiss her, I kiss her till she kisses me back.

LITTLE ROCK

Smelling bad,
Mr. Barrel House comes down the road
from the dusty sawmill,
ready to do it to Mrs. House.
Do it do it do it – that's his mode.

But she is a long time
removed from his mission!
Her shy children hide
in the old Ford in the yard.
Mr. Barrel House took his last whore
there, one night. Drunk, doing it.

With heavy eyelids, he came to my place
later for beer. Fell off the porch.
I sent him home to his wife and kids.

This summer, there isn't much work
in these parts. Men get restless.
The wives wash and iron.
And sing.

MATTHEW

Miss Brown, my woman, died
in a blazing fire in New Orleans, 1863.
Dumb child dropped the oil lamp.
I gave the child, a sick girl,
to Miss Harriet, in Jackson.

Went out to Wyoming parts,
became a bounty hunter with Joe.
Battle after battle.
Joe got shot in Denver,
cheating at cards.
White man shot 'im.

I spent six years rustling cattle
on a Texas–New Mexico track.
Today, I am old and out of tricks.
Never thought I'd cross back to
        the Southeast, but
can't stop thinking about Mama.
Nevada, though, is a hell of a way
from Waycross.

YOUNG WOMAN

Young woman – dark lovely angry –
old people are spending their last days
deep in your life. Your work is not a lark.
You serve them tea.
Yet they do not trust you.
You empty their piss pots,
and joy drains from your bosom.
I see you burn trash and eat sardines
from the can. You stand on the outhouse
throwing grain at excited chickens.
What kind of lady can you become?
Whores in the Valley knew your Indian mother,
the gambling drunks in town
were cheated by your black father.
Who are you? Where can you live?
Remember your grandfather's mule?
Left it to your father. Lost in a crap game.
The young mothers on the hill whisper your name.
Husbands are wild and helpless!
Still I love you –
and want marry you
and to take you with me to Denver.

THE SYNCOPATED CAKEWALK

My present life is a Sunday-morning cartoon.
In it, I see Miss Hand and her Five Daughters
rubbing my back and the backs of my legs.
Nat King Cole provides the music and the words.
It's 1949. Finished with them, I take off
on a riverboat, down the Mississippi, looking for work.
On deck they got the Original Dixieland Jazz Band
doing "Big Butter and Egg Man."
A guru has the cabin next to mine and everybody
who visits him whimpers something terrible!
Stood on deck after dinner watching the clouds
form faces and arms. The Shadow went
      by giggling to himself.
An Illinois Central ticket fell from his pocket.
Snake Hips picked it up and ran.
Texas Shuffle, who sat in with the Band last night,
      this morning, dropped his fiddle cases
in the ocean and did the Lindy all the way
to the dinning room.
I got off at Freak Lips Harbor.
Boy from Springfield said he'd talk like Satch for me
      for a dime. I gave him a Bird
and an introductory note to the Duke of Ellington.
Found my way to the Ida B. Wells Youth Center.
Girl named Ella said I'd have to wait to see Mister B.

Everybody else was out to lunch.
In the waiting room got into a conversation.
  with a horse thief from Jump Back. Told him:
My past life is a Saturday-morning cartoon.
In it, I'm jumping Rock Island freight cars, skipping
Peoria with Leadbelly, running from the man,
accused of being too complex to handle.
Sorry. Just trying to prove my innocence.
Meanwhile, Zoot, Sassy, Getz, Prez, Cootie, everybody
  give me a hand.
Finally, Mister B comes in. Asks about my future.
All I can say is, I can do the Cow-Cow Boogie
  on the ocean and hold my own in a chase chorus
among the best!
Fine, says Mister B, *you start seven in the morning!*

From

INSIDE DIAMETER: THE FRANCE POEMS

1985

AT POINTE DE ROMPE TALON

A woman sits on the one rock
white as her body. She gazes out
to the tuna-fishing silence
of the early morning watercolor
with its sloshing and response.

She is far away from herself:
not a hysterical uterine, not
Leda peaceful after flooring
the swan. Sea foam is not her
counterpoint. Sea motion is
not her metaphor.

DIVINE LAW: A BLUE BEACH SERMON

Women from Algiers sit
like white marble in their own darkness,
reaching slowly out for the weakest link
in an unchanging realm.
The holy government back home
cannot explain its bacchic shadow,
its nudes its maypoles. What do they hope
to touch, except another snake crawling
up a strange tree without branches?

Women of Algiers stand
in intersecting triangles
trusting the light of creation
to follow – shining through their dresses
toward the world of Emanation.

These women out of Algiers
are not really here in Arles expecting
horsemen to come for them.
The upper world
may open its gates. But will the light
shine down? In a landscape at sunset,
they wait for the call to prayer.

IN ABSENCE OF THE TREE

Sure, there is a hierarchy
of worlds here, one place
is above or below another.

Cap Roux is up the coast
beyond, say, Beaulieu
and below Eze.

Angels with dog-faces float
in chariots, spinning
through clouds on golden wheels.

You're not likely
to find the divine world up there.
Those carriages are on their way
to that place where earth

meets the world of action.
I cannot consult Ezekiel.
I'm confined to the speedway
along the blue coast.

Even if Jacob's ladder is dropped
it will not work. I am mineral,

molecular. Cells. Though I try
I excel at none of those systems.

So read Rimbaud to me.
Decorate my house with Baudelaire's
dead flowers. Roll me
in the sand at Monte Carlo.

HOME ON RUE DU BOURG-TIBOURG

Buffet gray marble with a deadness.
It's a frantic place aglitter with rudeness.

I give myself to it anyway.
It's a valley in a haze of Lido legs.
I take my coffee on rue de Rivoli.

Against the gray, red is intense.
Surfaces swell and crack.

The gray breaks and bleeds
into the frankness of red.

But don't think you've found a logical
extension of Expressionism.

BALANCE AND BEAUTY

We go over to see the head of a woman –
even more: night and mandolin.
One has to be right-
handed to get into the microcosm.
We slip in the back-
door: both working from the other
side of our brains.
At Port Lympia
nobody notices how skillful
I am at cracking crab shells
with my right hand.
Don't anticipate.
Up here, slightly above skyline,
nothing invades our rest
in the shaded cavities of this hillside.
This is no picnic at Saint Philippe.
The head of the woman remains
an unrealized objective.
In the village of Hélène
they ask why am I so sure
about this left-handed business.
I show them a map of my nervous system.
They say this proves nothing.

MONTALBAN: NEAR THE ANCIENT FORT

Hurry! Hurry!
Flames pour from the cottage window.
The plane goes down to sea,
and like a pelican
scoops up a beakful of water,
returns
to the burning vision
of a crucifixion which smells
of the artist's linseed oil
and the trapped mistress,
his muse, who lives in his throat,
content never to come out.

I watch the pilot pour water
into the artist's mouth and eyes,
and through his red roof. Yellow fire
eats the edges of his yard. The priest
has come and is waving a giant candle
at the anger of the artist
in his spilled moonlight.

Here too, an old peasant woman
with nothing to hide and her junk cart,
has brought sacks full of dead birds
and rotten apples in the name

of his color zone, as he requested
but no longer needs. As I leave him,
the artist is beating his way
across the hillside
with fire and smoke
swimming from the rear
of his musty brown suit.

REVELATION AT CAP FERRAT

It's not solely the dance
of the juggler but his spirit:
with its turkey wings, perfect thighs,
sensuous hips, large round flat eye.
This eye smiles like lips.
Watch this eye –
it's not a donkey eye.

It's not solely the dancer
who moves like a circus animal
as though to children's music – no,
it's the girl in the swing's rhythm,
the ticking of the clock at night,
the strut of the cock, the flight
of the holy family to the remains.
The nipple that feeds
the infant is an eye looking
into his future.

It's not even the village square
with its musicians and happy faces
that makes the difference – no,
because if it were, weddings
with violins, harps, flutes
would have settled the question:

no, it is the rising and lifting,
the failing and catching of
that unknown sense of self
before it crashes, that matters.

SEINE SPLIT

Maximum surge would place you
above your tolerance level.

Remember,
at that moment of waking,
your swimming body
divided into irritated halves,
one
floated up,
the other,
nude and undernurtured,
scattered as it fell down
insane and guilty,
pretending to be the lower twin
with the welded-in eyes of Gemini.

Paris had a way: it came
together as *content*
in one of you –
which one, I don't know –
and as the merged, reflected image
of Castor and Pollux.

If color were sound you'd hear
the bleak screaming of green.

When you tried to silence the conflict,
to yellow-and-blue it in dream,
it burned an orange hole
in your corpus collosum.
The brackets beneath your vermis
broke. Remember how silence itself
reached its maximum
in your central nervous system?

The Seine flowing through Paris
was the liquid that held
your two floating bodies –
bloated and bobbing –
in its stormy vomit.

DANCING UNDER THE STARS AT NICE

Are they sweating in the armpits
beneath the heavy wool as they dance?
Ask a dancer.
Which effortless colorless shapeless
dance is this? A friend
has just learned he has cancer.
He is not in the mood to dance.
There is no room left on the dance
floor anyway. Photosynthesis here
is not a process restricted to plants.
In the dancers' sweat
you can find inorganic salts.
Armpits may drink sunlight.
The motion of these dancers
is an act of biochemistry and
the effort itself makes use
of carbohydrates. Here near Old Town,
wet skin dries fast.
The shape of each step
is the nucleus of all motion.

ATELIER CÉZANNE

Blue chair.
We whisper.
Blue chest. We whisper here.
Dresser.
Here's the green apple.
A woman with braided chestnut hair
enters carrying green apples.
Here's a red one.
The candle.
Old jar.
Your top hat.
Your stained suit.
Your frozen garden.
It's like van Gogh's girl
against a wheat field: the wheat
is more important than the girl.
Things don't grow and express
themselves at the same time.
The bottle with the peppermint
I accept in its stillness, the rum too.
My eyes may swell red
and my fingers may grow thick.
I will die as you have died.
I will choose, at the last moment,
to see death in everything – in corn,

in flowers, in birds, and bats.
Your frozen garden is close
to the skyline that we call
the edge. We do not plan
to eat things from it.
It on the other hand eats at you
and me – and Vincent, too.

EN PROMENADE DES ANGLAIS

How would you have her?
In a metal dress
and with strapped legs,
as she hugs her neck?
As she waits for some guy
to come home from exotic
wild hair of women in desert boots?
Or would you have her
wear a left-armful of bracelets
that click as she walks?
Perhaps you want her on the floor
with her arms locked around her neck,
gazing suspiciously out of the corners
of her unbearably bright eyes?

Go on! Dance her in a Russian Army
suit or skip her high in velvet
and wool while her hair flops
about her shoulders. Pose her
in long leather boots. Call her
Bardot. Take her cigarette away.
Stick it in a holder.
Call her Lena Horne dressed tackily.
Let her run barefoot across the stage
at the opera. Take her out

on your yawl. Put a glass of Scotch
in her left hand. Give a dinner party
for her. Invite Lauren Bacall,
the Duchess of Alba, and Gabrielle Chanel.
There are many ways you can have her
and not go wrong.

ON THE OLD ROMAN ROAD

I'm doomed here at Saint Isidore,
in front of the little post
office, across from the butcher
shop, to fiddle and fumble
with my sense of the music
I hear. Swing me up
into the branches
and let me stroll the rooftops
while you, Jacqueline, reach up
with hands full of black flowers
to teach and reassure me.

From up here, I see across the Red Sea.
I enter the Great Desert of Africa.
I carry the tablets and tribal
scars on my face and the memory
of victory over the angel.

No!
I am not wedded to La Madeleine.
A dancing figure scratched
into the side of a black pitcher
with a crude handle.

Up here, I skip from cloud to line,
feel the growing lightness
of my ascent, then descent,
coming down I accept
our shortcut up the back way
back home to Route de Bellet.
So much is misunderstood
about my presence here
and I so misunderstand.

Jacqueline, you know
my motives, knowing
the old doc's works.

At Saint Isidore my hot flashes end.
Here suffering and dancing
are not quite equal.
Hard to tell audience from act.
The boy who brings flowers
to the older woman here
is not expected to lift
her body from her
permanent prayer position.

DRESSED TO KILL

They certainly do move
with grace, with great sturdiness,
these ladies of thin lips
in hats above uneven eyes.

They move without moving.

I look at their eyes,
jewels planted deep in skullbone.
They move them slowly.

I look at their necks,
necks as long as a horse's penis.
On the runway and in public
the women turn slowly, slowly
and they smile death warmly.

From

SURFACES AND MASKS

1988

I

and who must remain
stuck with the idea
that the Byzantine is "unlovely"
        or with the notion that
a "cultivated Negro" is necessary in a country
where one does not expect to find him,

                                        available
and speaking many languages, causing one
to feel ignorant?
        Had he been a son of North Africa
and not South Carolina – what then?
This Beloved Humorist
        on the one hand
could damn the Arabs
and defend the rights of Negroes;
step into Santa Maria dei Frari
        and feel outrage
in the entranceway. And why

was the gondola black?
Behind every closed window
on the Grand Canal, Othello and Desdemona.
The threat of cholera, then
        hung like fog on the surface
of the page, in the end being itself

a signal –

     vast signs of poverty, many
beggars begging – insisting really
on their own serious anger…

Thomas Mann. Thomas Mann
was impatient with the closed windows,
the smelly streets,

        did not imagine Desdemona
but a boy white-shod, "at once

            timid and proud,"
a boy, Mann's boy – and not Bordereau.
Giovane as the Fountain of Youth!

… something about Venetian girls, too,

     having sweet and charming
and very sad, oval faces.
And wasn't there something about

        an underfed
look? Well, I never thought of them
in those terms…

To take a posture – "I quote the principal

       parts,"
"wave-washed steps" (to quote James,
to quote myself), seeing this place

     as a getting-away place, away

from the hardness of plastic edges
            and the sharp surface
of every secure thought I ever had,
is, in itself, a conspiracy

        Left to rifle the situation
I'd hang them all in San Marco
like the French conspirators
            were hanged
after the Plot of 1618
            was uncovered.
Then console myself with the music
of Schubert and Miles.
They?

Her face was framed by
            a halo of thick dark hair.
She was no doubt a contessa, (they
        all are!)
        and you could see the distant signs
of Asia around her African eyes,
        the Middle East
in the slope of her nose.
She was the summation of the human race.
        Her seriousness was Greek.
There was no way to point
        a finger at any part of her.

In her knit stockings,
                she walks
arm in arm with another girl.
       She parts with the friend
and calls back over her shoulder,
           "Ciao, Anna!"

       She is the dama Veneziana
of the 1720s,
           complete with hooped
                 silk skirts
and a black velvet cape
which is attached
      to her jewel-studded crown
and reaches nearly to the floor.
She carries in her left hand
       a gold cross
suspended on a circle
           of pearls.

IV

He gave the Fascisti salute
     when he stepped off
the *Cristoforo Colombo,* 1958...
       there would be, I knew –
if nobody else ever knew – an endless
              Sordello;
and poor "Eleanor" and all
the dream-dreamt Grecian faces
       I could scare up,
the cries in the nightmares,
     the Acaetes-announcements;
everything you can imagine –
        least of all,
that worn-out, "Hang it all..."
      and
    and... worse! One could get hung
       endlessly up in it all.
I said in my attempt to clear
          my mind,
    "Goodbye So-shu!"
and I was waiting,
     on my way,
not even mindful of night
       whisperings:
    "Past we glide!"

There were those
            willing to introduce me
to O.R., but she was too old,
        and therefore
the conversation was likely to be
not worth the trip, but –
            on the other hand,
there remained the quest
                for kissing:
"Kiss me as if you entered gay
        My heart at some noonday."

The gondolas always –
        repeat always –
cost too much, any year.

I was either a guilty traveler
                from or to
"glorious Babylon" or else
        I was less wise,
less concerned
            with these surface effects.

A deep echo of Disraeli,
        fearful of my plight here…?
            at sight of cemetery
lying there in mist, I drew

back, sharing Disraeli's fear.

    Can you imagine yourself
wandering into a late-night bar
               in Venice
wearing a mask – even at Carnevale time?

      We bought the papier-mâché
         and covered our faces
   for fun, gambling

on our luck.
    (The Serenissima, in these days,
        would not try us for it –)
But
poor Disraeli! "I fear I have no title,"
     he said,
"to admission within these walls,
      except the privilege
of the season."
     Only in a psychological romance!
But then you try to find a way out!
     Or you wait
and listen to Countess Malbrizzi,
    who asks,
"Shall I tell you
your name?"
and you know

   damned well
if you let her
you are going to end up
in bed with her, ah, making love,
    or worse!
   And once you are with her,
close to her,
   in her arms, you are obliged
   to not only let her tell you
your name, but to let her melt your snow.
   Mount you?
   Warm you?
As the countess
   she will tell you
she has the power to dream
    you away,
to turn you into a ghost,
    make you
part of the city, fade you.
   And you will be quick
to warn her that you have never had any
   "sympathy with reality."

Then there's Dickens.
   "So we advanced into the ghostly city,"
   and Dickens had had no idea
of what he was talking about!

The proof is that he went on:
"…a black boat…"
one of "mournful colors…"
moving
silently through the night.

(I saw them
all day long, mainly – which proves
nothing.)

Yet something in you
has to go out
to that old boy, Dickens!
"So we advanced
into the ghostly city" – of
death death death!
Poor Dickens!

VIII

and as the memory of each
                    hard melodramatic word
laced my mind
              I heard (thoughts
of Shelley's Ocean's nursling
                      plus)
the language pitch
          of this
       "woebegone population";

in other words, was this still
such a place? of "blearness
                    of scrofulous children"?
in a landscape of draggle-tailed
                    pregnant women?
I didn't think so.
     A different enchantment
now held.

IX

There he was, a boy, looking over
                    the canal
at the hostile area with its grandiose
                        structures.
It was years later
            that he thought
it unnatural they locked the gates
            (closing them in) at night –
prisoners in their own beds.
        Why should he ever want
to go over there?
        The boys threw rocks at them.
Everybody he felt safe with
            wore yellow hats.
Heathen roughs wore no large Os
                    on their breasts.

The day before Dead Day,
            we are on the ship
to Torcello – happy,
                bright and warm.
Brief and sweet.

Saw contemporary paintings
        at Palazzo del Diamanti.

The one of casanova soup
suited my innocence best.
P. favored the winged crudities.
Search me!

Went back to San Erasmo
for the fiesta – this time
it was sunny
and they had ribs.
Didn't stay for the breakdancing.

Must take the ferry
from Alberoni to Pellestrina
because
everybody says we must.

Man scrapes rust from *fondamenta*
rail all
morning. Paints it black
after four.

M.L. came down from France.
Spent three nights.
Wonderful, seeing her.

On the Lido again –
Winter sky. Coffee

outside. Via Negroponte
    and Gran Viale Santa Maria
                Elisabetta.
Girl misunderstands
    my misunderstanding
regarding the lira.
Later, walked on the beach.
          Breeze, sharp green
and gray.

Dreamed about the Festa del Mosto.
    In the dream, stayed for
          the dancing.
All of it –
    Manifestazione
    Regata mita
    Spettacolo
        etc.

To the train station
    to buy the paper.
Lonely and cold, the weary
          children
of all Western nations
        sit
on the steps with the birds,
    gazing at the boats

going by on the Grand Canal.
　　　Backpacks stashed
by their legs.

　　　They sleep
in the protective coves
　　　of quiet *campi*
　　　　　and grand old churches.
If winter is not here yet,
　　　it's coming –
and fast.

Seagulls scream
as they circle
the fish market.
　　　The fish seller
laughs and throws them
　　　　　little sardines
and innards scraped out
of the larger fish.
They swoop down,
fighting over the gifts.

The gondola riders look up
　　　insecurely at windows,
not trusting the trip
　　　they are on.

In darkness, they drift
    silently along – wildly
drinking wine from the bottle
    and
      slapping
each other's knees.

Smells of fried fish
    and grilled steaks
at outdoor table
    across from Piazzale Frari.
Italian lessons, anybody?
Signora carries her boots
    till she comes
to a puddle. There, she puts
      them on and
walks right through
    like nobody's business.

Girl takes off shoes
    walks barefoot
      through, while
the anarchists come
    to Venice
wearing cool irritation
      like suede boots!

The tour guide has a bright scarf
        pinned to his hat.
The group follows the scarf.

Signora brings the chicken
        back to the butcher,
sticks it under his nose,
        commands him
to smell its rotten odor.
Swirling feather falls
        from sky in front
of the school of birds.
                "When I went back
to America I was shocked
        by the sound of cars."
"*Gondola! Gondola!*" – the mournful
                                call...

After the rain, the canal water
        rushes along, tossing
the boats violently against
                        embankments.
In the afternoon,
        the city is sluggish with humidity –
a heaviness made more
        of silence than air.

A sudden, hard clear sky!
     My head clears in
     the strong morning light.

Japanese tourists
     armed to the teeth
with cameras go by
        under the window
in a string of gondolas.
          On TV, Japanese
cartoons in Italian –

Graffiti – as history:

Signora sits on chair
     in restaurant, waiting
for hard rolls and creamed coffee.
Her feet do not touch the floor.

Water level drops low
                        in the canal
and the stink rises.
            My knee swells
and the foot shrinks

                    and Poe's man
            cemented in a wine cellar wall,
                    at carnival time; you see,
            "There is such a thing as being
                        too profound.
            Truth is not always in a well."

XII

The theme of Carnevale is a secret
                                              this year.
You have to guess; play the game!
          The mystery is the main
                                              thing.
You do see various variations
          of classic figures:
Doctor of the Plague
Bauta
          Rotunello – in baggy pants
                    carrying a string
                              of sausage
                                        – from Roma,
of course.
          And kindly Bertolado
on donkeyback. He comes here
from Bologna… with:
          Dottore Balanzone –
                    serious-minded fella,
                              this one.
He spills red wine
          on his white collar;
takes his cape off and places it over
                                        a puddle
so that native Signora Rosawra

may cross. Others –

      Lucinda, Isabella,

            Flaminia –

follow her lead.

      Poor Dottore Balanzone!

        (Meanwhile, nobody

puts down a cape

      for Colombina

to cross the puddle on.

      Faggiolino suggests

she take off her apron

      and spread it over

         the water.

The crowd laughs.)

      And those from Bergamo –

Brighetta, first.

         A pirate with a long

           twisted nose

and a dagger in his belt,

      he'll cut your throat

         for two hundred lire

         or less.

And Scapino,

      in blue. Well dressed.

         Yank his cape.

      And Messetino!

      Pluck the strings

               of his guitar!
Dance with him, in
his red-balloon outfit.

Arlecchino –
          harlequin, spotted
and sporting the feather
          plucked
from the tail of a green-headed
                              duck
that has come on the wind
               down
from Siberia for the winter.
          Introduced by Goldoni
                         himself,
the spectators cheer.
          Only one Bronx cheer.
That overall is a good reception.

Now,
          Bagottino
               in black mask
                    and white shirt and pants.
Meo Squacquera (from
               Calabria) with sword
          dangling
from his hip – mouth free

                    of the long-nosed mask –
cape flying behind him
        as he dances violently
to a music imported
        all the way from China.
        Then to music from Spain,
        where the bulls
used to come from.

Proud – unmasked – Lelio,
        native, leans on his cane,
                                watching
Bagottino and Meo S. make fools
        of themselves.

Little Captain Spaventa (of
        Liguria)
struts about
        with hands on hips,
                cape dragging,
feathers in his band
        so long they dangle
in his face.

Playful boy yanks Glanduia's pigtail
        and he loses his Torino cool,
tries to catch the culprit

but the kid is
a breakdancer
who has developed
a running ability
equal to the East Bronx's
hellishness.

You will take a sip
of the brisk wine
Meneghino offers you.
He comes from Milano
with the kegs on his donkey.
He drinks to your health.
You had better drink
to his, too.

If you meet Patacca
in a dark *calle,*
walk sideways, and pray.
And these ones from the South –

Pasquino
Pulcinella
Scaramuccia

What can I say?
Dance barefoot with one,

tap your walking stick
            with the other,
exchange knickers
        with still
                another!
Clown! Snatch a skullcap
                        from a dwarf.
And the natives –
        Pantalone,
        bearded and caped
            Florindo –
        like a French madame
in riding britches – carrying
        a proper crop.

And the others –
        Stenterello:
                funny-faced guy
                in orange vest
under his blue suit.
Firenze accent…

Tartaglia – of Campania.
        Dance with him
                at the ball.
His yellow stripes
        will dazzle

you.
Dance with Pugantino
               balanced
on your shoulder.
        He will enjoy
the ride.

Then when the formal parade
        has passed
you realize how relaxed everybody is.
        Nobody pushes.

But nowadays this is the way
                              it is:
Under a flimsy pink parasol,
        held above his head,
he walks proudly
               through the *campo* –
a black silk mask
covers his face.
               Tucked beneath his silk
hat, and covering the sides
        of his face, a piece of old lace:
unless you know his walk
you cannot guess.
He holds the hand
        of a clown

with a big red nose.
You snap
their picture.

Carnevale is not
yet defeated, though
it's raining cats
and –

XIV

Little places.

      Corte Stella.
    White sheets hanging
          on clotheslines.
Flowerpots
     inside barred windows.
Broom propped against wall.

      Rio de San Barnaba.
   Gondolas.
      One half-sunken,
filled with snow.
On the other side, little boats –
            sleeping birds.
Their bodies reflected
   upside down in the water.

Rio Terra dei Catecumeni.
     Windows covered
   with a profusion of blooming vines.
       Winter sunlight
    in spring.

XVI

We climbed the hill to the carriages
     but saw how the royal family
          down
          there
          behind us
drove in, slowly,
no doubt
feeling great and proud,
     as they approached the castle, yet –
going on, up and in,
     we laughed at the funny ones,
and admired them all,
     all of them with wheels.
It was a day, an outing,
     and the food was worth it,
although
          I splashed snail sauce in my own eye!
And the ambiance was all of it.
After the big Easter feast,
     in a crowded room,
we went out and sat on the grass
     and I sketched
the village in the valley below
          with
its mountains ranged beyond.

But all of this was before
        the carriages: queen's,
                king's, gent's.
Then we came down,
        bellies still full, and feeling
grand and humble, not minding
                not getting into the villa
                here at Maser
where Veronese painted the walls
        with hunting scenes
for the wealthy family, not minding
                and
minding a little bit anyway,
                sad and happy,
fretful and calm,
        we drove back
to Venice, our city of canals.

XVII

In Salute again.
      This time, did not feel
burning from arrows shot
into neck, chest, stomach, thigh.
I bled though, but not much.
      To fight pain I kept
          in view the woman
across the room; she's from Orante.
Her passion is sad.
      Distraction is good for pain.

Out to Torcello again.
      Hard spring! Light
high and sharp, higher noon clear
      with shadows deeper
         than direct,
and beneath us – hey! – the Antichrist
      on his throne
holding the c.c. on his lap.
      Not exactly the way I
              remember
it, the fire
and angels poking heads
      you might have thought
good or at least worthy

                    of ascent,
                                down
into the volcano.
            Out there there are levels:
                    skullbones (finished)
                    people waiting (to burn)
                    the half-burned
Lucifero in his inferno!
            The woman from Assunta
                    at the other end, trapped
in mosaic, unable to move
                    even
                    if she wanted to
lift a finger –

The light in San Giorgio dei Greci
            is not the best, yet
you reach up through it
                    to touch The Passion
in the Orthodox manner
            with its seventeenth-century
                    red-gold yellow-gold, but
your fingers fumble instead
                    upon the eyelids
            and across her nose, blindly
guessing appearance.
Faith in art restored,

you go next door
      and into the arms
of the woman of Hodigitria.
As though you really were her child,
    she makes you
       look toward the camera,
tickles your belly,
    tries to make you smile
      but too many centuries
of suffering the sins
    of the Judeo-Christian human heart
have turned your little head
      and its quite odd face
to metal quickly painted brown.
    Here in Ellenico
there is a stillness, tender
    but not soft enough to soften
your hardness.
    Your fingers, chubby and little,
      play
with the stone-hard creases
       in her dry-blood
       red robe.

XVIII

You set out on a morning bright
            for the guild,
as though you were an invited guest,
        about to take part
in some important civic discussion,
            and
        who knows,
            you might do just that,
                                after all.
Here in the Scuola Dalmata, the caretaker
            mumbles to himself
pacing between the card rack
        and the entrance to the upstairs
                        room.
        Darkness is cold, and the only light
comes from the static voice
                    of Carpaccio's...
George is calm, almost bored
        as he drives the spear
            into the neck of The Uncontrollable Forces
of Nature.
You think he is probably too late.
        Look! Look at the destruction
            he's already responsible for.
Yet you see among the half-eaten

bodies, skullbones
of other animals,
       so you know you are not up against
              a discriminating beast!
His fire – like the fires of Hell
       heating the furnace of Heaven
       at the Ellenico – is also ironic.
George could not be more
                     connected
to the dragon than he is
       by the straightness
of his spear. The serenity behind him
       in the land and the sky,
even in the straight still trees,
       and the bright little buildings,
and in the calm water of the river
       (more a medieval Tuscan *virtú*
              than Venetian!),
       are as much
                     connected
to the dramatic turn of events,
                     the sharp
abrupt lines created by George's horse,
       the spear, as to
the bleeding dragon,
       George himself.
And this is where the discussion

begins.
But what you are not aware of
                is this:
a lion has followed a man
                        into
the *scuola* and when you turn
        and see this for yourself
you know why
                the others who've just gathered here
                are now running in every direction –
some upstairs,
        others toward the door.
The Lion-Man is old. He uses a walking stick
                to walk.
        You see the caretaker's fear grow
                        as he trembles.
A group of monks
        that has just entered
                turns
and returns to the *fondamenta*.

XXII

In a blazing sunset
                    the gondola
moves silently along
                    the surface
of the lagoon, like somebody
        sneaking up on Sleeping Beauty.

Green ducks fly up
                    against the light,
electric as shock
                    from some invisible crevice,
and they are caught
                    in midair
by my own wonderment
        and remain bright
as dandelions
and as tentative as cats
        on the *fondamenta*
after a storm.

XXIII

and the single reality
      of the closely lined buildings,
casa after casa,
          reflected,
like a young man's convictions
              (shaky,
upside-down, blurred,
      like yellow-and-white flesh,
are somehow steady
      and understood, sure
as the hand of a housekeeper
      who has been
with the family
      for nearly a century)
is a reality uncelebrated
           except
in bad photographs
      by determined tourists.

That's how important
      the long dark point
of this simplicity is.
      Is there progress?
Do you mean, uh, toward recognition?
      Yes, eyes about to open to

the occasion, and it is
      bending with the wind,
where everything suddenly
      might be seen,
as it breaks with a snap,
      and the joy of it,
transformed as understanding,
          stays on clearly
      centered
and smelling like sap
      from a young branch.

XXV

See that stern castle?
It was once
           a great old whorehouse.
Now, all alone, empty,
     closed for centuries,
no boat anchor; it's unmarked.
      It might even in some ways
be seen as a lonely casa
           in a graveyard,
for over here, on this side
     not far from the cemetery
the merry daylight of death
        is always waving
its tear-stained flag.
             Still,
vain, dreamy, defamed
     and the victim
of a lost fortune, this place
     is a sentry
to the flesh-grinding profits
       of the pirates
who smiled beautifully
     and lived filled with noise
while trying to avoid the Bridge
        of Sighs.

Stout women once leaned
                              out
of those windows
          purring like motorboats,
                              waving to sailors
passing below
          in narrow boat
          after narrow boat –
long slender nice-looking narrow boats.

If we were to glide by
          now,
                    very close to the dock,
we would hear the echoes
          of an enchanted though bruised
                              life;
peculiar in its solitude, while
          thoughtless
in its sentimental enthusiasm.
                    As we go by
out here, far from it,
                    without moral peril,
          in our vaporetto,
                    we are travelers,
far too far from those decorated windows
          to catch even the ghosts
                              of kisses thrown,

for centuries,
        down
                from them.

XXVIII

The old woman comes
        along our *fondamenta,*
                Tolentini,
every morning around nine,
           dropping sardines
along the way with
          the cats trailing her,
eating the fish. Lucky,
          these cats.
Those in the Campo San Vitale
                  suffer
especially when the construction
      workers are not working
on Ponte dell' Accademia.
And when it's finished?
      It is winter, already.

XXX

They cut down the last tree
            on the *campo*
                   where I sit
near the old boatyard at San Trovaso.
         The birds also miss it:
                  they fly into the space
where it once stood and
                           sink,
        as though in quicksand.
I can now see the path,
                     church,
       and castle.
But did I need to?
Rain now
          falls hard to the ground,
with no leaves or limbs
                 to pause on.
Yet, when did Venice
           seriously
        need trees or gardens
              not secretly
kept behind stone walls?

XXXI

The canal, this one,
                    was dug at the turn
of the century. Beneath
           the *fondamenta*
           are the logs
and mud
        of an incredible handshake.
No sharp shadows
                 are left. Buildings,
          dynamic yet so elusive
they might be illusions,
                 in winter light.
Space unnatural?
        Over on the mainland,
                    at Mestre,
          a redundant green
     wind, high
         whipping dresses
             against thighs.
Cemented drain carries water
                 on down
toward the library
        but not quite that far.

XXXV

Alone, I went into that special
                    little windowless bar
near Rialto market,
        said to be the oldest of its kind
in Venice; ordered –
            with exaggerated ease
            (like an exhibitionist
                bullfighter
waving his muleta unnecessarily) –
                        a *tocai*
and began to eat the sausages
        from the tray,
just like the regulars do,
        attempting to feel Venetian.
It didn't work.
        The fish at the end
                of the line finishes itself
by pulling against it. The bartender
        overcharged me
as though I were a tourist.
        Had I not lived here
a long, long time?
                    Then I returned
            a week later,
quite by chance,

with A.,
who's very, very Venetian,
classy and quick.
We had our *tocai*
and sausage together.
Two fishermen in the alley
outside
were laughing happily.
The bartender gave me,
like a present, his biggest smile.
I felt the Great Blue
River running through my veins.
I was a way
I had never been before.
A. and I had our *tocai* again
and the bartender
insisted we have thirds
on him.
With a light head
and happy at noon,
I walked home the busy way
and found P.
making lunch.

XXXVII

A Venice dream of the mainland:
          shocked out of night
by morning, in a skiff,
          on a duck stream,
my tongue dry, swollen,
     as from the air
in a torture room, I stand up
in sleep, looking up
     at the zinc dome
of the sky, I try counting
          the flock of geese
exploding overhead.
     I have about as much luck
doing that
     as I have trying
          to restrain the mad dogs
barking at them
     and running upstream.
Then I woke to the sirens
     of *acqua alta* and the dragons
          known very well
to be reality.

XLIII

In the hidden garden
　　　you force perspective
on us
when you push us to flowers
　　　where flowers are
already crowded,
　　　losing their aromatic
ability to whisper names,
　　　names like

　　　　　Miranda
　　　　　Luigi
　　　　　Orlando
　　　　　Pasquale
　　　　　Valentino

or kick back at us,
　　　creatures
no stranger than they,
　　　　　　in groves
along the stone fence
like this here
　　　　　in warm lagoon air
　　　　　　　　rain-wet air,
　　　like the rooftops

                    beneath
which we spend
most of our time.
            But your garden is special.
                You force us to stand
firmly
        against the only space
        your flowers have left,
while we, sporeless,
                            rootless,
        seasonless, have other
options. Why then do we weep
                before these flowers?
Let's gather their camphor scent
        with their roughness
and stickiness to our bosoms.
                If you have a camera,
click fast because we are
                    about to move on
and may not return
                for a long time.

From

SOME OBSERVATIONS OF A STRANGER AT ZUNI IN THE LATTER PART OF THE CENTURY

1989

LOST IN THE DESERT

I

The sun,
      in her memory,
          held itself high
above its bed,
      the mountains – to the south.
Human bone, beaded dolls, chunks
          of turquoise
were the relics of her cove.
The "Coral direction" pleased her,
      looking down that range
to the sound of *tesese* (once she
          tapped the taut skin
herself and heard the power
          of sound
lift up from the orifice).

Her throat dried faster than the pit
of a clay oven when
          the match
is struck to paper
          beneath the wood.
In silence, she turned
her small emery wheel.

In silence, in silence.
The sun
      disappeared
behind the range like a prairie wolf
entering
      a path through desert rock.

She was out
      here now (in the music).
Her heart was a terrified cactus wren
            gripped
in a dirty fist.
            Unseen Hands was not there
to protect her
      from the Mystery –
          and its danger.
He's a gray fox –
      they're in a desert
and she's a desert rat.

            In the mirror
she sees the beginning
      of the full moon
and more – herself as windstorm,
          as summer flood,
          as migrating coyote,
          as spotted skunk

on the run;
as sheepherder
rounding up strays,
cutting cattle
for the Nastacio family...
It was the summer her brother taught
her to fly
like a bat –
(instead of eating
the mutton she fed it
to the wild dogs –)
and like the other things
that came while she slept.

"You look like you
just saw a ghost!"
Somebody in the desert
was frying pork chops.
She could smell
the smoke, blue as leaves at dusk.

He spread the blanket
and made the fire.
She concentrated
on the radio static
in her chest.
Once in a while in it she heard muskrats

and wolves sniffing
the air in the cliffs
                above Zuni
        where the clans
                had their summer
                                feasts and dances.

The sun
        in her memory
was going to be her moonlight
                all this night long!

II

It gets very cold   here
                        in the valley
below Sacred Mountain…
                Her father proposed
to sell her to a richer family

        … so she could eat.
"I told him I didn't want to eat."
        So she eats with her fingers,
chili stew…
The cold made the hunger worse.
        She stood between two
beehive-shaped ovens
                        in the yard.

In protest her mother
        refused to pack her clothes
so the father had
            to do it himself.
"My grandma told him the BIA
            was against selling children.
Zuni law wasn't,
        he said, against selling."
        She put on her buckskin,
                    moccasins,
ready to go.

The shouting?
        She ran, stumbled –
fell into the catfish river
        got rear-ended up
the stream, grunting like a Coronado
                    pig,
broken like a Coronado horse,
            the dyes washing
off her skin
        as though she were an olla
painted with mudfrogs
            not so carefully
and with the wrong stuff.

III

Stiff, by the light of kerosene,
                on an orange crate,
by a clay pot
                with mudfrogs and delicate
                                plants,
also this – turned the wrong way –
                this arrangement
by the bed… She saw
                        a young man looking
                down
up-
        on her, waking.
He said, "Unseen Hands
                placed food before you.
Eat."

        Up, back against wall,
the platter of catfish
                on her knees,
still her hunger didn't reach out
        to it. Of more interest
was the lighted side
                of the wide face
                                above her.
"Who are you?"
                He made his sign,

his fingers, little *hapas*

    with the corpse-demon heads

you expect.

    IV

About the desert,

        she whispered

like a Ramah Mormon peeking

      into folded hands.

    Not from the terrace

of an old house, not by a fire-

             place

while using frybread

      as a spoon in stew

or a wrapping for the catfish,

        her father…

about this desert – the opposite

      of "my people lost in the lake" –

    she whispered in a clearing

halfway between Saint John's

      and Surprise Valley,

as though she actually stood

    at a juncture between

the Colorado River and

      the Zuni River north

        of Hunt,

smelling brush burning but

                              with no sight
          of Sacred Lake. Nothing about this
          desert reminded her of tomatoes, melons,
                                        and peppers.
          She whispered with awe
          feeling herself sinking in sand,
                        as in
                water, dying, consumed…
                              Thought about guilt,
                  poverty –
                        of the ancient ones,
          all those hundreds,
                hundreds of measured times,
                                        coming
          down from the mesa
                        (for no clear reason,
          as they had gone up for none).
          If the infants became too
          troublesome, why
                              wouldn't the ancient ones
                                                drop
          them in a lake?
                ("In our belief
          these children who *fell*
                        in the lake
                became the first kachinas.")
          They live down

at the bottom, and come
up at night   and dance
      in the plaza.
Not always friendly, these –
      You could be left
a bleeding victim of one's rage!

Which way, this Sacred Lake?
At Dowa Yallane
      it was never mentioned.
Nothing about it and nothing
            about the desert either…

But it goes on – memory, sound,
      all of it, the scrapings
on wood, the turnings, moonlight,
            sun!
The help of Unseen Hands,
            seeing a way through
windstorms, all of it!

Out here, one needed to learn
            to be as untrusting
as the coyotes. Yes,
      moving the way they move;
            carefully.

IN HOLLYWOOD WITH
THE ZUNI GOD OF WAR

> *... movie people. They all seemed quite mad.*
> – *Peggy Guggenheim*

I

"It's as fake as Zuni
                    jewelry made in Taiwan,"
        I heard him
                tell the director
and that he was Zuni,
        and to his disgust
in Culver City
                cops called him Chief.
I was playing a mysterious dark role:
                                not a speaking part.
We were in the Cochise movie
        and this is what Zugowa
                        pointed at,
as he spoke.
        The director said,
            "Do ya wanna work or not?"

Clowning, an Italian dude playing Cochise.
An Apache guy on the set
        told the director where to go.

148

Nearly got us all fired; set closed.
　　　Producers came down, frowning.
　　　The script was all
　　　　　about the capture of Cochise.
Zugowa and the Apache tried
　　　to point out to the director
　　　that he should start
with the white men whipping
　　　old Red Sleeves –
　　　　　Chief Mangas Coloradas –
because that's where Cochise
gets his anger, his motivation!
Talk about motivation in Hollywood!
　　　　Director told us all
to go get laid in Burbank,
　　　"Whatta ye guys want?
　　　Ya got Studio City by da balls!
　　　Ya got all the blonds
　　　in the District hot fa ya
　　　'cause ya born widda suntan."
Anyway, Coloradas struck back
　　　and the white men killed him.
　　　　　Shot him in the back.
They say the whole
　　　　Apache Nation rose
　　　and this is where Cochise
of the Chiricahua comes in,

but the director

wasn't interested. He started his movie

with a bunch of Anglo cowboys

galloping galloping

across

a phony Southwestern landscape

raising a cloud of dust

trying to track down

Cochise.

Cochise, you see, before the flick

kicks off, has been accused of killing

little Micky Free

(we never learn that Cochise

is innocent,

and later, that he wipes

out forty before capture.

You see two fall).

I saw Cochise hiding – Zugowa

said, "There, away in the hills,

but why isn't he holding them off?" –

till he's captured, but

you don't see the army losses;

you instead suffer

like the ache in Big Eyes' knuckles

when he drew maps for Coronado.

II

It was during the time when
         everybody was hot and bothered
            by that Mexican laborer
               who killed this Indian
over a quarter
         which the Indian dropped
            in a jukebox
         to play an Elvis Presley song,
            in other words –
You know what he said?
"What ya got against Elvis?"

Zugowa was in one about
         a stagecoach robbery.
I sat on the sideline singing
         about Dat-So-La-Lee, watching,
            chewing sage to keep my breath –
blessed *polienway*! – Yuccasweet.
         All the Indians were wiped out.
            I saw it in L.A. – without prayer meal!
The audience loved it!

         I was in the Tomassa one,
            Zugowa wasn't. I got shot
in the first scene. A daylight person,
         I turned into a Shutsina –

Zugowa was in that Pocahontas
    (silly, silly, silly…)
             thing.
A remake of forties sentiment.
        ("It cannot be helped;
    we do not have the same
    road," Bunzel quoted Lena Zuni.)
Yo-a!
      No *tcakwaina mana,* this
Pocahontas! Break the piki
    in her honor! She was good,
said the Anglos, 'cause
    she saved the life
of one of their own. Two? I forget.

"They did not care
        which tribe we came from."
Zugowa swore this was true
    in the name of Awonawilona,
             by his own *mili.*
To them, we all looked alike.
    Being herded and shot
paid better than oranges
    in S.D. County,
or the H.D. in Arizona – that is,
    if you could get yourself shot
at least once

per month.
A liberal producer
        from back East wanted to make
a flick on Cherokee Gatumlati till
        somebody told him she was half-
Negro. Studio pulled the plug
                out of his oxygen tent:
        white audiences in the South
might not buy it.

You might think that because Hopoekaw
                was married to a French officer
she was safe territory, but –

        Hoooooooooo thlaiaaaa!

Me and Zugowa tried to get the director
                to eat *etawa* and *yepna*.
He left our table gagging.
        Heads in the cafeteria turned,
faces turned red.

We offered him queens,
                Cofachiqui and Pamunkey
                and royalty – Adell C.,
        and twisted the arm of Joe Tipp,
                the token,

but got back "how
many times" etc., and the business
about "point of view"
and audience demands.
"Flick like that won't fly!"

III

… and this Navajo hombre said
why
did the Navajo
need a Bilagaana – must have
been Kit Carson's face!
or did your ancestors screw
that many blue-eyed settlers?
and the black gods?
What's with the black gods –
Bitsiilslizhims?
And you say we shot down
our black savior!
He was no savior, Saiya!
You drink too much!

… and he said, We had Yellow Body.
Calling God.
Toninili.
Water Sprinkler.
Zugowa had a friend at Saint Anthony's

whose name was Bilagaana.
Imagine that! Know nothing
about Blue Body. You keep thinking
"me" some kinda studio-lot priest!

(... bartender is sympathetic.)
Ahhh, the curse of Haashcheeshzini
is henceforth upon you!
"Ready?"
"Yes, yes! Altseasdzaa!"

IV

Ooooaaaioooo!
Hoootaa hooota!
... the movie about Sacajawea,
the so-called Bird-Woman of the Shoshones.
You
know the story?

"... but they [Lewis and Clark] would
have lost their direction
without a compass."

Mother of Chief Quahhah,
Cynthia Ann Parker,
of the Comanches – was proposed
to the director by a group

of intelligent feminists. He shaved
      his finger at them.
They got the point.

Zugowa and me farmed out
      parking cars in South
L.A. when the Emily-thing
        got the okay
from the lot office.
      This jerk-off lieutenant,
who's obviously been pumping her,
        marries a girl of the garrison.
Poor Emily, poor, poor Emily!
      Emily, the stupid Indian
      "gal" who's shot by a sentry
as she sneaks back
      to warn the garrison of a planned
          Indian attack.
Last straw!
      The director told us
we were fools to
        jockey autos for peanuts
and tips from the crust! when
        we could ride high
      in the saddle under the big sky!

A GALLUP SWILL-HOLE; OR, CANTINA BLUES

Her words curled before him in spirals.
She told him, "They work
a section-gang down the street."
She, Sheba, the Navajo,
never spilled beer.
"My folks are of the [censored] clan."
Her words sped in jerky motion.
She told him, "We left
the reservation when I was ten.
I lost my [censored] when I was eleven."
She went to wait on another table.
A guy slapped her big fat [censored].
A bunch of dudes from Black Mesa Mine
still in hardhats came in.
He admired the way she handled them.
Her words curled around their heads,
turning them back into farmhands.
She, Sheba, the Navajo,
punched Hank Williams's "Lonesome Trail."
She took the empties away and
never once let on that she felt
like [censored] every minute here
with these ex-sheepherders
in McKinley uniforms.

TEWA VICTORIES

The Town Chief fasting for rain,
a procession of singers walking
              from the desert back up
to the mesa
        with the little wooden man:
                              Saint Augustine;
a lone man carrying a cross
            slowly,
        down from the mesa to the desert;
        another planting prayer sticks;
one cocking a rifle,
        one a sack on his back –
going out to plant seed
        and chewing the root *ballafia*…

            and the condor comes
down with a lightness
on the roadside, hops to the body
        of the dead skunk.
Something whispers from the crevice
                in the sandstone
        five miles up the canyon.

So the story begins
        without a story intended.

He now fed a clown piki.
He imitated a woman sweeping
                        a path
for the Mapuride; he broke all
        the rules when he helped the women
make mudcakes and wrap them
                        in cornshucks.
He himself was the Mapurnin.
He handed medicine to the mayor.
He expressed with hands
        and face the agony
of misunderstanding between
                a reservation cop
and a personator of a kachina.

The laughter was sincere
when he wiggled like Chu,
                the Snake Kachina.

He shook a yellow gourd
                and kept step
in the circular Christmas dance.
In January he joined the Laguna dance,
        wore the evergreen
branches around his hips but
                the execution
        of the eagle

the day after Home Dance
gave him guilt
        he scrubbed furiously
like a dirty hand.

The mayor speaking Tusayan
congratulated him on the room
      he added to the house
his ma and pa still shared.

He gathered berries
      and passed them around.
The people were tiny, stiff,
       and grateful.

      One year he was Kapyo
                  coming up
out of the roundhouse kiva,
throwing a spear at a deer, then
he went out and brought the evergreens
      back on his back.

His father weaved the blankets,
his mother made the clay pots.

He danced himself crazy
      in the Pinitu fertility parade!

When the woman came
      and asked to be whipped,
the mayor chose him to take up the whip.
She was sure his beating
      would drive out her demon.

He decorated the Kekei Virken.

He kept us in stitches
      when he became a coyote
trying to chew
      a prayer stick
    from the ground.

He ate a *natoai*
      with more dignity
than any other Hopi.
In the foot races
      he ran faster than roadrunner.

He got his friends to help him
      plant *thlawashie*
in the Painted Desert – to make
an altar of stones
      where the spirits
could live.

On All Souls' Day
      he went with his old ma
to the graves where she dug

                a hole

at the head of her father's
      and placed in it
a few bread crumbs.

He broke a bowl on his knee;
      left it on his grandfather's

             grave.

Then back up to the mesa.

He made a circle of candles
      stand
around a bowl of corn.
Slowly, he lighted them,
      slowly.

He was chosen to take the sack
      of corn down into the kiva
of the War Society.
      He did it well.

Without touching his knees
      to the ground
he buried an ear of corn

        in gratitude
to Great Mother Earth.

They all said his Shichu
               dancing
tore roughly at the wind
          and that was very,
                    very
good – better than his coming
    up
        out of the earth,
all alone, as Haukabede,
with such an innocent,
          decayed white face.

He spoke the words
        of the *hakuwam*
as though it were a cluster
        of hanging yellow flowers!

As Black Eyes
       he did a two-kiva strut!
As Red Eyes
          he disowned the taffeta
a girl pressed into his hand.

When he was too old to play
                    Aiyayaode,
he taught his son
        (except the part where
your cock is supposed to leap out –
                    innocently bouncing
from one thigh   to the other).
He liked his son best
            as a Thliwa dancer.
On the first deer hunt
        his son took,
he taught the boy how to chew
        a piece of venison and suck
in the breath of the dead deer.
He was the Hunt Chief.
            He carried a wolf fetish,
and dreamed all day
        of rabbit stew.

As the Clown, he carried the willow
                            limb,
red as Red Eyes' eyes, running
            holding up his yellow limb.

He taught his son
        how to use the figurines
in his wolf pouch; to smoke

out the rabbits hiding
        in the desert brush;
to throw the *koa*
            at the fleeing rabbit.

All his life all was well
        till his wife died
and he could not find another
                young one.
When he went to an old one
                for her yes
she told him what was best.

SIGN LANGUAGE

Lift your left hand
like this. Higher.
That's right.
Keep the fingers together.
Palm down.
This informs the world
that you are not afraid of flying.
Now, interlock fingers of both hands.
This motion commands
the universe: it means
life is life. Okay?
Beat the palm of the left
hand against the right.
No, harder. Like this!
You know what this means.
This time, hold a level hand
flat against one eye. Yeah.
Look sharply out
of the free one. Get it?
Learn to sleep
with your gloves on. Make sure
the fingers can move
within. Wiggle them.
Keep them warm in this way
all winter. In the spring,

give the gloves to a hawk.
Somebody else will need them.

NEW AND PREVIOUSLY
UNCOLLECTED POEMS

1958–1998

SAVING JUST THE REAL

When I was born I saw
death devour the birth
of something, perhaps
the first thing so deep
now it's hard to say,
fruit perhaps, peaches
on my mother's table.
Then the particular way
chickens stood
on one leg. Death
in sparrows. I remember
their closed eyes,
the hardness
of the body of death.

1968

FIRST

A woman is sitting in a doorway
of a thatched-roof house.
Paul is painting her as part
of the background
for The Great Tree.
Up close, I realize the woman
is my mother and she's in a trance.
In the single eye in her head
she sees the wall
that separates her life
from her death.
Her first memory is red
and cold, wet and cold.
Her last is like the first.

1976

SAND FLESH AND SKY

Our ropes are the roots
of our life. We fish
low in the earth,
the river beneath runs through our veins,
blue and cold in a riverbed.

When the sun comes up,
the moon moves slowly to the left.

I tie the logs and limbs together,
holding them in place.

The ocean beats them
smooth like rock.
Here my sense of time is flat.

I find in a strip of damp sand
footprints and marks of hands,
and torn pieces of flesh.

Night is a beast.
The tide moves, gushing
back and forth.

Sunlight touches our faces,
turning us, turning us, turning us
in our morning sleep.

1976

PENCIL SKETCH

Smell of rain in the air.

Sunlight moves
over the cornfield.
A lean tree shades a cabin
      at its edge.

Figures bent digging,
      hoeing, planting.
A young man stops
to stroke his sideburns.

A sheepherder herds
a flock on a hillside.
Behind the hill, a forest.

Heavy rainclouds coming
      this way and
light moves on toward the hills.

I'm a tired city person
who has stopped to watch.
Dust from my tires
lifts high over the field.

The forest grows darker.
A figure steps from the cabin
and rings a cowbell.

As the farmhands move
        toward the sound,
I try – with my eyes –
to hold a stand of trees
still on the horizon.
Fire burned away
all their leaves
and now they are ghosts in
the mist of the coming rain.

1978

RIDERS

The girl was riding a horse
alongside brave hunters
with painted spears.

They jumped fences,
following loud, barking dogs
in search of boar or wild turkey.

They camped.
She went out in a boat
with two. Downstream.

From there they saw the blazing
fire against the night cutting
mist along the mountain line.

With its ears twitching,
a mule deer stood in a clearing
in snow near pines.
His head slightly raised, sniffing.

  1982

POSING

They've forced me to pose
in the picture with them.
I'm the unhappy one
standing next to the man
with sixty miles
of summer in his smile.
Like the others,
I'm looking at the camera.

Now I'm looking
at the photograph to see
if any of the fifteen
of us has been, magically,
moved out of place,
shifted forward
or to the side,
changed in any way.

Why are we posing?
Because there is
terrible faith
in the ill-equipped future.
We pose for the conquest of it,
to keep the setting sun behind us,

to assure the photographer
that we believe
in his belief in us.

1984

ROUND MIDNIGHT

You know my story.
They want to make me liable
to punishment for this picture.

So my spirit is closed.
I'm a delicate engraving
outlined
with semitones, curled
at the edges,
nearly worthless,
in mysterious trouble.

I walk the beach
at Scheveningen.
Drink myself blind in The Hague.
Piss in the bushes at Etten.

I redate all my efforts.
Reconsider a cluster
of old houses nearby,
but not the church behind it.
You know why.

Midnight is round.
Asleep, we go around in it.

So what if I fail
at the total – the whole?

Judith Te Parari
couldn't care less.
She swings low
in her sweetness
around midnight as
the diggers dig
the fields stacking mud
against gold panels.

When I come to trial
you will hear
in my defense, weavers
and rug makers, potters,
old men leaning on sticks –
people I trust – tree cutters,
tree growers, folks born
in the month of March.

In Harlem or Stuttgart
you can make anything work –
jazz with hard light
against the Rhine;
even a tiny red boat
tossed this and that way

along the tired face
of night's season.

You know the story.
I am held captive by winter light
at Nuenen next to an ox,
hooked to a cart, hopeless
in its sincere effort
to go on and on.

Judith holds the end
of the winter thread,
pushes it through the needle,
then through my lip
and through midnight and
sews me and it together.

My spirit rises. I drink
nectar from her Nefertiti
moon. It's midnight, exactly
and I hear – what piano keys? –
not from Rick's. It's the sounds

of water at the Gennep
Mill, turning, and
I am a monk, waiting,
holding a gift –

a token of reprieve
placed in my hand
by my defenders
who also wait now on
benches harder than mine.

1984

STUDY FOR A GEOGRAPHICAL TRAIL

1. Seattle

The neat sky was tall, full of sliding birds.
I was sunk low in the wet trees,
surrounded
by brown grass and butterflies.
I had no castle to look at.
I was out of my mind.
Without tenderness, I was out
of breath. In my memory
the city continued to tease.

2. Illinois

A man shot at me. The bullet missed
and hit a veal steak sandwich
my friend was eating. The afternoon
turned dark. What else is new?

3. Washington, D.C.

Don't lose any important papers.
If they can't trace you to paper
you're lost. When I traveled alone
in foreign countries the officials
discovered – before I did – that

I did not have arms. In Tokyo
soldiers laughed at the holes
in my head.

4. New Jersey

So much depends on four butterflies
waiting quietly on a stem,
moving their wings slowly.
I wish I had wings.

5. Maryland

Sunlight here is hazy. Builders
made everything the same.
I've got fair weather but the high-rise blues.
Shopping center on one side,
dog run on the other. Give me rolling hills –
not Dulles Airport!
Where is the silver spring promised
in the name? Yes, the weather is
fair – but what is unfair is the climate.

6. Boulder

The terrific sky is full of birds
in formation. A girl's hair dries fast
in the light. Snow disappears in thin air.
To protect itself from pain

the population pretends it is lighthearted.
Gangs of deer stand at the roadside
watching Dodge vans.

7. Alabama

I am leery of old men in suspenders.
They smoke cigars and listen
to Lawrence Welk. I want wings
to go up with the birds.

8. New Jersey

Forgive me, dear. I ate the five
women you left at the kitchen table.
Their clothes were bright.
I knew you were saving them
but they were so cool and tasty.

9. Chicago

It was summer at the edge of town.
Two men shot at me.
Bullets flew through the park.
A woman fell.
People gathered around her
and ripped her clothes off, tearing
at her dying. Stretched out
on the ground her sobbing shook

her pink pants as the grass turned
from bright green to red.

10. New York

I am running, wingless.
This is my chance.
I move – as a plumed serpent –
through the airport.
I want my hobbyhorse.

11. Boston

Be careful inside buildings.
People paint dramatic lines
above their eyes in the toilets.
Women chew gum at typewriters.
Relocation camps are hidden
in basements. The lights
make you crazy. There may be
no single good eye left.

12. New York

Restless people gather
under the sky, under gliding birds.
Hands are up. Hardhats walk
in the rain. To the left,
the traffic is sluggish.

An army helicopter goes by
overhead. The white fence
is the border. A broken red
wheelbarrow rests against it.

13. Atlanta

At night during the war
I watched a movie of a woman
taking a shower: one arm
raised above her head – she
washed under the raised one.
Such big hands she had.
There was no fig leaf
between her legs.

14. Denver

Forgive me, but I must stop
to eat. My important papers
are in my vest pocket.
The restaurant is quiet –
only one other customer: an old woman
with thin red lips and deep
blue circles around her eyes.
Plump in a dark red velvet dress,
she sags against her worn fur
coat. The rings on all ten
fingers sparkle.

15. Alabama

I am leery of ladies
in white dresses. They tend
to come down steps too gracefully,
heads held erect, wearing flat white hats
with tiny knots of flowers stuck
to their sides. What is unfair about this?
The space behind them is
left blank.

16. Mississippi

The fine sky was wide but
I was unhappy with the horizon.
Scrubwomen wearing red headrags marched
in a graceful single file
into the tallest building
at the vanishing point.

17. Texas

One must be especially
careful in the open: birds fly overhead.
The space behind them is crowded.
Clouds form into the shapes
of a woman sitting on a bidet
cleaning herself after a customer.
He is dressing – pulling on his suspenders.

18. Vermont

In the afternoons before the war
I posed for a painter
interested in showing how
an outsider looks against
a sensuous background: the park,
the town, the naked ruins.

19. Nebraska

I brace the drill
against my rubber apron, watching
the metal shavings spin
out around the point of entry.

20. A State of Mind

Finally. Waking, the head
contains a sky as clear and blue
as a hangover. Trees shake – thin
yellow fingers frozen in the wind.
The light beats my body, shakes it.
Turning around in an unexplained space,
I tremble in the delicate power
of my own visions.

1984

190

THE OTHER SIDE OF THE WALL

1. The Women in the Waiting Room

This is the image: an old woman in a blue hat
with a smile at the edge of her mouth
and a light in her light-brown eyes.
Forgive us, forgiveness. She's near
the window of sunlight stillness;
near snow-covered silence;
near muffled traffic.

An even older woman here in a funny old hat.
Suspicious eyes. A thin line for a mouth.
A long hooked nose and sunken cheeks.
Face of unforgiving anger.
Returned greetings come
through a painful hardness.

> *Standing in stream she bends,*
> *gathers her skirt hem into delicate*
> *hands, squeezes out*
> *water and blood.*
> *A front curl falls*
> *out of place, to cover left eye.*

Young woman in yellow
stands against white wall.
With shawl draped loosely around her shoulders,
she holds her right arm
across her stomach.
She strokes her chin
with the fingers of her right hand.
She watches the two old women
as window-light changes on her pinkness
and in her blue eyes. It turns
her dress gold. She clears her throat.

> *In the temple she is running*
> *from the murderer. Everything echoes!*
> *Light from the outside comes in*
> *along the walls, across the floors.*
> *Screaming women in long gowns,*
> *carrying infants, run barefoot*
> *into the main lobby – from narrow hallways.*
> *The murderer flies among them,*
> *swinging his sword! Heads roll,*
> *screams die in blood-filled throats!*

2. The Operating Room: Emergencies

The doctor waves his baton;
he comes out dressed as a large kid
with an all-day sucker.

The head nurse spins a yo-yo.
The band whistles encouragement.

The women are waiting, doctor!

Behind the doctor is a busy city.
Darkness, in gray. A sprinkling of light
plays against his now-serious cheek.
His assistant nurse enters in an Hawaiian grass skirt,
carrying a ukulele in one hand, and
in the other, a fistful of St. Elizabeth's knives…

The curve of her spine is deep!
Her strumming is slow – a sound
of meditation, a whine!
The women are waiting, doctor!
The door behind her is of black chalk.
Image of the women waiting still
sharp: lips closed, they watch
floorboards.

Doctor, doctor! He's in short pants
with a few front teeth missing.
The waiting room is full – !
He wears a mask – the Comfort
of Tears! There's no traitor

in the butcher shop, no actors
half-in and half-out of light.

> *He was the captain dead overboard,*
> *the rest – naked on a raft shooting*
> *downstream!*
> *Pregnant, with lumps in their breasts,*
> *they could not turn to him.*
> *The storm was furious: a single sail*
> *ripped from the pole.*
> *"The operating room is ready, doctor!"*

The first patient is escorted in;
her hat is removed.
From the other side of the wall:
weeping, screaming, vomiting!
The doctor and head nurse – face to face:
his hair curls up and out.
Eyes: black dots – hers: moons
full of water. His whiskers:
rear thighs of the porcupine.
His hands shake in the shipwreck.
The Coast Guard will never come.
He wants to take the blue hat
from the nurse and wear it;
dance snow clouds around
the operating table. He rushes

the patient; giggles at her fear!
"Forgive me for what I am about – "

3. In the Storage Room for the Dead

The widow of the gravedigger
is not looking at the man
who is looking at her.
His eyes are slow, unmoving –
large and gray. Has the French nose.
She too. They are caught
in the stillness of an embrace.
She's waiting for the right moment
to wash the blood from the skirt.
They share the guilt
of the emergency – the spinner,
the sucker! Yet not lip
to lip: not eye to eye,
not cheek to chin: he juggles
a dog, she a bird. He cuts
the mother open to release
the separate person.
Light shifts
on the backs of his hands.

The widow of the gravedigger
has plucked eyebrows. She looks
constantly astonished; she turns

the doctor's fingers back
as he strokes her bottom lip.
A breeze in the lobby feels
like the thirteenth century.
Instead of slapping him
she remembers his face above
her the last time he reached
into her with both hands.
Left eye: dead as a doorstop.
She fluttered beneath him,
half-alive – a bleeding bird
shot by the archer. No Madonna
ever was half as empty,
as her womb closed.

> *She is dressed to the neck;*
> *hair covered to the hairline.*
> *The thirteenth-century doctor*
> *loves this about her: such contrast*
> *to his bloodstains, untidy hair,*
> *his mask!*

The gravedigger's widow
does not mind the doctor.
She did not mind the gravedigger
himself – the mud on his boots,
his sack full of bleeding rabbits;

his filthy, drunken pub talk;
the way he kept her waiting – !
She did not care
about the doctor's dirty collar,
his bad breath. Even the salt
of his kiss was sort of sweet.

1982

BERNARDSTON

Where?

– James Joyce, Ulysses

I

Excuse the unromantic place –
a few miles north of Greenfield
where wind rips yellow leaves
from October. First time here, in
an old hotel with closed bar downstairs.
The mythic figures of literature are far
away. Cows, I see, grazing on hillside –
above them: the sky. Epics have no place
here. Listen! It takes a hillbilly two hours
to drive down to the post office for a stamp!
Ash trees as symbols are things I taught.
Now these sharp cold days, filled with steam,
in the room, are for reading
and making love with my wife.
You'll find us at the intersection
of Massachusetts Highway Five
and Highway Ten – fifteen minutes to Vermont.
From here to there, they're closing
roadside stands. We bought the last good tomatoes.

2

The white Fittonia veins in the green surface
seem even but they are not. A profusion of leaves
in the shade, by the window, seem still
but the steam is moving them. The long shadows
of fall – in here and out there – are cool
and vacant yet I *know* them, as I know Cézanne,
to contain life! The sun on the Fittonias –
it is moving fast. Their veins glow white!

3

The hallways are dark. A midget downstairs
uses the public toilet on the second floor.
When he hears me coming up he peeks
through the door crack: one big red eye glaring
with a retarded blankness. We came here
from a different kind of life. I do not
understand the midget: yesterday
across the road he sat on the back of a donkey
in the shadows of an oak near the liquor store.
The whip rested across his shoulder.
His short legs hardly allowing his feet
to reach the rings. His posture and mood
were the same as the donkey's.

Nights, the roads are dark and foggy.

4

The metallic red, yellow, and green
of the TV screen glows before us
in the warmth: back view of a woman
in pantyhose; men in armor; seated figures
on a front porch; news of murder;
an election; of the best deal in town;
the dark areas around the eyes;
soft, wet, glowing sensation; still
life with flowers; hard and clear
fences; everything you can imagine;
the bone beneath the cheek; red lips
light and wet; pink body-color turned yellow
with chalked-in outline, finished
with a fine brush. Edges
carefully worked smooth. We grow sleepy
before this magic.

5

In the dream I am worried about the furnace:
I had to keep the fire burning or else!
Nobody liked waking up in the night,
trying to dress in the cold. Most of the guys
in the barracks were from cities
and had never seen a furnace. Yet they
stoked it too when their turn came.

After feeding it I returned to my bunk, to sleep –
for an hour. I slept at the edge
of a cliff, an arm dangling. The flames
were still yellow with red centers
at six. And my relief did not show.

6

The coast isn't far. After a few days
all the leaves are blown from the trees.
The stairway remains dark; and we hear
the groaning of trucks at the intersection.
I go on gazing at the Fittonias;
glancing at the midget's inscrutable eye;
watching TV's bigots and hooded mystery.
Then we are seized by a lust to drive.
To get anywhere we must drive.
In the thickest fog
my wife follows the white line.

At the coast the wind tears at the sails,
overturning small craft; rocking even
the big boats. Women in long dresses
walk with their heads lowered, pushing
against the thrust, their capes flapping
behind them. Hats fly out to sea. Barefoot
children run in the current.
We hold each other, trudging through

the wet sand. *Man trying to anchor boat –*
rope breaks, boat tossed out beyond recovery.
His little red coat beats furiously
against his back as he watches.

Coastal dreamtime?
"Serious" winter holiday coming – proof:
a holy figure scratched deeply into the surface
of a rock. Her lines are old. On her knee,
two infants embrace. A tear rolls down
her cheek. My wife and I embrace.
"I think we should buy a beach ball!"

My wife bends forward against the wind,
her jacket flapping in the storm.
She sits in the tide and watches the photographer
snap picture after picture of the surf model. I watch her
watching them. She is not Phyllis
in search of Aristotle – not a symbol.
The hotel in Bernardston is not the castle.
Wind nor sea will take her.
She has no miracle to reveal.
I am not a figure in action.
She is not Venus.

7

Back in Bernardston I dressed in blue
armor – charged forth with my sword out
before me, ready to strike! Symbols, epics,
mythic figures – caught up? Think not. I stood
halfway between dream and the room. Clear,
here we were safe, though still
dislocated. Sword? Unnecessary!
I came out of the "forest" and stood
at the intersection of Five and Ten.

8

It's late. We are two lovers
in a meadow up near the border.
The sky is yellow. Blue potato cart
near the gray fence. A ladder lies
against the haystack. Vermont is prettier
than Massachusetts. We kiss. Five figures
carry a dead cat on a stretcher
between the olive trees. Moonlight
shows them to be mournful.
They let the cat down into a limestone tomb
at the end of the yard where the flowers are.

1982

THE SWINE WHO'S ECLIPSED ME

I, the alleged culprit, have a case.
I, the alleged captive criminal,
deny these very words: this
is a tirade against my own claim,
my existence. Hold these words
up to light, they will burn the page.
A Machiavellian of moral poison,
he holds my arm twisted
behind my back. I know
of no forthcoming parole.
My one chance is to reach out
and wrap his neck in confetti,
then crawl out through the tail end
of my own metamorphosis.
Yet I hear the action: the poison
arrow I drive into his heart
may be my own first step
to pushing up tulips
on a grassy mound.
We pay the toll as one.
Drawbridge guards do not tax us
as two. I, the alleged salient spirit,
am the true wise one; I am reliable,

moral, able to catch myself
even before I am thrown.

1989

LOVE AGAINST DEATH

I

Night odors: wet grass, wet trees;
sharp smell of skunk and roses.
Night sounds: outside the window:
burp of frog, the shrill instruments
     of crickets. Death,
she said, is the double cross –
in wood. There it is: in the ring
and splash of sunlight.
I want to pour mud into the sun
and jump the Wall of China. But
the moon drives me
to self-reflection – especially as it
comes through the window now.

Life is possessed by garlic and
the madness of Estelle, crisscrossed.

2

You stand in the yard, yours,
feeling crisscrossed, possessed.
Touch the whitewashed wall.
The rooster starts crowing at three.
Walk on the damp grass, you see
shadows crawling in front of you.

206

3

While waiting for Father Divine
and a miracle, my past lives with us.
The magic in Mineola placed him in
the powerful silence of maids
and white women from Canada.

In memory of my past – and in self-
forgiveness – my wife reached out
and touched her own broken leg.
It was a clam with a Universal Mind.
The long years of my history
grunt in her and my ears.
My black spats turn silver,
my brown derbies blue.
Welfare-check windows fill
with green smoke.

4

Estelle. Estelle was mad.
She was the aunt who raised me.
Life was overtaken by her Christ.
Whatever self she danced
before me was a widow
        of Death.

5

My wife and I now walk
through fall leaves.
What we say is reflected
upside down in the pond.

6

In the night, between the odor
and the sound, we hear the train.
It passes beneath a flexible bridge
with walkways on sides.
Without being down there, I know
a girl in a long white dress
watches it from the rail.
Though it's midnight, the sky above
        her is green.

7

The skunk comes by the window
two or three nights a week.
The boys come in and roll
the bed out into the sea.
I usually don't wake till
the dream of infancy ends
and I'm falling out the cradle.
I want to pour mud

into the cradle,
once and for all.
I float back.

8

Death, she said, is not all
she's cracked up to be.
She's a little muddy and flat
with bark for a bed.
A harlot, perhaps. Something
tangible to look at.

9

With our love, dear, we fight death,
and we fight unclear meanings.
They are like air released
in a broken scream –
at three in the morning
when your legs feel wooden.

Embrace night odors.
Embrace each other.
Rub your hands
against the roughness
of the whitewashed wall.
For now, you are alive.

1982

APPLE CORE

Up the road
I saw blackbirds
on the edge of a pine box.
When I got there
the birds flew a few feet away,
to the other side.
I looked down in the box.
There were red apples,
ripe, with stems still on them.
A sign on the box said Take One.
So I took one.
My, it was heavy,
and when I bit into it,
you would not believe
such sweetness. I walked on,
eating it down to the core.
When I finished, I threw the core
out over a cornfield.
A bird flew to catch it
before it hit the ground,
but it fell anyway.
The bird followed.
And I stood there,
not seeing anything
but the stalks moving

in the morning wind.
I waited, and the bird
came up, carrying the core.
He flew off across the field,
carrying this thing,
about twice the size
of his own head.

1990

HONEY DRIPPER

Savannah, Georgia, 1902

Little arms ripped out
of their sockets,
belly devoured down
to the backbone
while Honey was at work.
How could a dog named Eddie
do such a thing?
Sheriff said it was her fault
for not feeding the animal.
Is there such a thing
as food for thought?
"Had no business leaving
them kids alone nohow."

Honey Dripper, Honey Dripper
(whose legal name
was Eartha Romance)
had three children –
Mona Lisa Romance
Paul Romance
Molly Romance –
all born under morning
stars and out of wedlock,

and each to a different
silent or lost father.

One's dead
and the other two
they say are out there
in the State's hands.

1992

FRENZY

Here is the little earthworm-eater,
she-kiwi.

She's in her frenzy of lust.
There she goes in her flightless

night journey, in mating season,
warm in her fur-feathers

poking her long bill, beaker,
with nostrils at the tip

sniffing and drilling
scratching and uprooting

with her powerful feet
pausing, maybe, to let

herself be mounted
furiously and briefly

by a he-kiwi whose
odor is to her liking.

Then there she goes again –
through the underbrush

(followed by her
faithful seducer)

back to her *querencia*
to burrow down

and wait and sometime
later she stands up

suddenly, and hatches
a big egg

nearly half the size
of her little body.

Finished, she steps away
and the father-to-be

steps in and sits
on the egg

warming it,
sits and sits warmly,

for three months
while she-kiwi, lustful still,

goes out looking
to get laid again.

1994

WYOMING

I drove north, lost
in Wyoming along a river.

A sun-dappled day, I was moving
by looming blue mountains

dotted with pine. Through
a thousand-acre spread

below a retirement village
way at the top, I drove

past highway-boys
vanishing in clouds of dust

while looking for downstream fun.
I drove past hunters in dugout canoes,

moving like wildfire on water
and on I went still lost.

I swung around a gang
of Whitman's bare-chested men

logging timber, then
I stopped to watch

a mutton-busting ride
in a cow town.

They had banners stretched
from bank to barber shop.

A river of red cattle
pounded through town

and went winding up
a narrow road.

I ask a cowpoke
for directions while he

held a lamb
between his legs.

With big shears in one hand
he looked up and said,

"Back where
you came from."

1994

TRAIN STOP

The train stops.
I'm trying to remember the name
of a woman at a train
stop like this years ago
who said she was possessed
by demons she called Enslaved Selves.
Gave them names
like Toxic Tamalina,
Malignant Majesta.
But wasn't her real name Karen
or was it Karla?
I gaze out the window
at the city's lunch counter
lights, wondering why
it feels like I've been here
in some sub-zero past stuck
in time – nickname and all.
Through the window
I see a railroad-crossing bar,
Sam's Diner,
and beyond, a run-down town,
one with nothing coming –
either way. Two tow trucks
are stuck in mud.
A green light stuck on green.

The stillness is unfriendly –
dangerous as an uninspected dam.
I see the shadow of a woman
coming across the tracks.
Her name might be Karen.
Remember myself saying,
"Nice meeting you.
Hope you dispossess your… yourself – "
and her correcting me,
saying, "Selves," and, "Thanks."
Very rational. On second thought
her name might have been Karla
and the city might
have been Santa Fe
or Savannah. Caught
between foot trails and
foothills, it's hard to say.
I've lived a long time
and made about as much
impression as a polypod
on the rest
of the hope-and-grope garden.
Karen? The train was coming.
Red light stuck on red.
What I have to say about Karen
can be said in my last days
in the rest home

half out of my mind
on the sun porch
at midday midafternoon or midway
of a game of pool in the rec room.
She was kind, civil and kind –
and very rational. As sane
as any of us. Saner, underlined.
But will I live that long?
Surrounded by shady rock-walls,
spruce and sweet sedge
with a blue-eyed nurse taking
my pulse between her quick
cigarette trips out by the
whitewashed wall. But most
likely that other Karen
will be somewhere too,
with her memories of
having slipped her enslaved
selves off to places like
Saginaw and Sacramento
releasing them, like little
birds tossed up set free to fly.
She will watch them
huff and puff, up over the
yucca and the yew.
They will beat their motorcycle wings –
crotch-rockets hit by a windstorm.

But don't count on any of this
or the special symbols:
emotional ports of entry,
lonely airports where she
might be spotted, telling her story
to stranger after stranger.
Don't count on seeing her
on a ferry crossing over
from the mainland to the island,
or next to you on the train.
As I say, the name might be the same
but the heartbeat is purely individual.

1991

UN POCO LOCO

– for Bud

To start, I have to draw blood,
find the right weakness,
show my grief,

just to get things moving:
sweep a bit,
dust my broom,
and since what I'm after
is so abstract, I bump
hard into chrome,
into the cluttered tables.

This one nearly killed me:
a lover I never wanted
to see again, a half-empty
glass of wine, lipstick
stuck in its brass tube,
a Cupid nailed to a globe,
half of an apple.

To keep going, I think
disconnected thoughts:
Chatter. Chew-tobacco.
Phoenicians. Rednecks.

To keep going I watch
my grandmother hold
the chicken by its legs –
bauk bauk bauk!
Chuck this time.
Cluck-Cluck last Sunday.

Keep going – the work
is the person said Peter
and proving it standing
there like that, silent,
before two hundred people.
That's one answer, the work
itself. No time to stop.

There's no time to stop –
for sickness or Jim Dine
or clever lines or the
upshot or the right note.

No time to remember
precisely – two glasses
left on the floor by the two
of us, gone down to
the level of plant life,
where we look so mysterious
and lovely that nobody's

going to care whether we
sprout next spring
or not. This is the problem
with a complete thing!
You can't lead it away
from the water it wants to drink.
It will kick your brains out!

Nazis drew blood a certain way.
They started something
they couldn't finish – they nailed cupids
to crosses and fed apples to snakes,
raped on the Riviera
and kicked holes through the dance
motion of abstract paintings
I expected to see later in Budapest,
where leaves on trees, birds on skies,
played Bud and whispered
Monk intimacies.
Take three. The Nazis
would have been better off
up in trees by Blue Lake.

The Pawnee is not going
to get nailed into a frame
of the Great American West.
Custer points his six-shooter

at the Indians' back:
only white space, the page's
margin between them:
the gun goes off:
a fluke of Nature: I bleed.

Take four. To start again
the light has to be just right.
I'm going to shoot the scene
before me: here –
Phyllis with that calculating smile!
And perhaps your brother at
the piano with polished fingernails
making bobwhite sounds.
Start again.

Take one. There are no miracles.
Take two. Being a little crazy
isn't the result of a
volcanic eruption.
Being a little off,
places you in touch
with Jene Ballentine's
Born Free, 1968,
with Whistler's gray and pink,
with lava and its flow.

Let's do it again from the top.
It's not Art Deco,
not locomotives of
brilliant returns
from sparkling cities,
the polished nipples perched
atop Byzantine temples;
no, no – it's the return
to the unanticipated
start that continues to count:
one two three – Go!

Sure, I'm electric.
My colors remain pure.
My columns won't shift.
Variety keeps the boats adrift.
Blue Lake absorbs the blood
and flows on, still blue.

1991

IN WALKED BUD WITH A PALETTE

T. Monk and P. Cézanne: Cézmonk

(Alternate take)

Take one Pompeii-eyed old man
with a brush, poised in midair
near Mont Sainte-Victoire,
take one strange young man
filled with light,
bopping at the piano
        in Minton's.

Who are you, dull-eyed
mathematical seer?
Who are you –
monsoon-sound maker?

I force the two of you
together – mix you
in a blue bowl and
you rise like a Blake fantasy –
a vorticism unto yourself,
left-handed with keys and brushes.
I call you Cézmonk.

I hang upside down from
your gut-wrenching rafters.
Birdcalls go out from you
before sunrise, combo-smooth.
They smooch the sky.
Your boats are filled
with labeled gunnysacks
of precise beats, licks, and
uncoiling cubes of careful color.

I'm knee-deep in fidelity
to what you see, to what you hear.
Ruby, my dear.
I'm lost now, T, in your
bright armpits of tangled vines.
I'm lost, lost now, C –
Ruby, my dear,
Ruby my dear.
Yet I linger lost,
mixed – short of breath,
in your tall darkness,
waiting for your next move.

Tell me –
what's your hidden agenda?
I've made you a tempest
pretending to be

a dog-headed storm.
Surely your agenda is not
the spreading of Greek
creation myths, not
the spreading of grapes of Paradise,
not the churning of bodies
in cotton beds, not the splash
of church bells across the village,
not the smile of a patron
saint of brick buildings.

You say you created me –
you should know my agenda.
I know that light dances
in cubes like bop piano notes
across Lake Annecy,
North Carolina, where half of
you rose from the water.
Oh, Ruby, Ruby, my dear.
I know the smell of a hazy day
of gathering weedy flowers.
I know the sound of flowers.
I know you are anything of life.

I gather myself like flowers.
Your trees look back at me
like hungry animals.

I am a chimp eating termites.
I swim back and forth
between your two shores.

You are Gilgamesh's buttons.
You are toes of a Spanish martyr.
You are teeth of a vestal virgin.
You are purple rocks in a stream.
You are ghost figures in a zoom lens.
You are seeds in sunflowers –
      in that vase on Vincent's table.
You are the interior of a dolphin's mouth.
You are the unoiled screws
      in a new motor.
Your sounds and colors
    are my self-portrait –
unlike me, it's
a portrait of
uninterrupted elegance,
an elegance twice that keeps
lifting lifting –
lifting belly to the dice-
thrower behind the curtain.

   1996

BEING AND BECOMING

The parking lot was
full of cars full
of dead babies and
thousands of court summonses.
Then is now.
I squat in the lot,
looking at myself
in the hubcaps' silver.
Oh dear, beneath the bright
artificial lights nothing
is simple or clear.
I see and see myself
in the pigmented tinsel
and the yellow chrome! –
and trust what I see.
I felt sure of myself –
was able to approach
my own alloy-plated
identity! – that great
American wasteland! –
with some sense
of chronic calm!
And I stood up and
cupped my eyes
peering into

the nearest car
and after that
I gazed at them all
car by car
till I understood that
each infant death was my own.

1990

THE STRING

My mother tied
a string around her finger
and just as she was
trying to tie it to mine
my sister ran off with it,
tying it first around a tree
then a bush, then
around the house
and up through
the moon and back.
By the time
she returned my mother
was old. She yanked at the string
as though it were a plant
in dry earth.
I picked up the string
and took it from there.

1990

UNWANTED MEMORY

My memory of myself
has become a drawbridge
to ancient catcalls
left echoing in my brains.
I was the victim of a jihad.
I pause before plunging in –
once inside there is no elbowroom.
Inside me
there's a catatonic ape
trying to get a grip
on his mate and his failure
is respectable without
being a violation
of Nature. It is not
like working for the film
industry: he does not
simply plug along for fear
of not getting another gig.
Part of the script has to do
with a churning mixture
of bad memory
and using one's finger
when the dike is about
to show its tendency.
Not to blame, I forgot

what I was going to say.
Oh, yes – see this window?
I'm going to take it,
unscrew the frame,
and ram my head through the glass.
I will march with it
around my neck like this
along the river down
to the drawbridge and stop
at the dike. Here,
I will have no trouble
remembering what to do.

1990

DANCE FLOOR

Bone-thin gent
in waistcoat and tight pants,
struts to stone-staircase music.
He is a saddled camel,
stepping high in high-top
shoes. This caravanserai
belongs to a fancy age
of waiters in bow ties,
ladies in bloomers
made in Palestine!
The genesis of his dance
expresses itself
as he kicks the ceiling
while turning cartwheels
for the Queen of Sheba
who watches him from
behind her Phoenician fan.

1990

BRICKS AND SLEEP

In late afternoon,
the first row finished,
lined up neatly end to end,
with mortar still soft
as tree sap between them,
you start the second row,
cutting no slack,
staggering them firmly.
Night, you barely sleep –
still busy stacking
things now you can't see.
And in the morning,
with coffee cup warm in hand,
your bricks are hard
and you're somehow rested,
despite the busy night that
hums like motors in tanks.
Skin fresh to cool breeze
from the south, you start
your sawing. You're cutting
all morning, cutting two-
by-fours, then cutting your beams,
then cutting your planks. Now
you dump a keg of nails out
on your tarp like somebody's

stars spilling in a pattern
across some deep black sky.

In the afternoon when
the sun is too hot you go
upstairs and lie down, reading
a novel about a man
with a rake farming his own
land and you spill into asleep
transplanted to his land
where the soil is moist
and, like his, your hands are brown.
When your work is done,
you enter a dark hut –
like a cove – and
you build a fire
and with care, warm
those same hands by
the potbelly iron stove
you find there.

1995

A SLOW PROCESS

It's a slow, slow process.
A clumsy male

milkweed caterpillar
is turning itself

into a butterfly.
It hangs from the underside

of a withered leaf dark
among a pungent cluster

of rich leaves. Just
hangs there as though

it were not changing
at all. But at a certain point

in its natural growth
caterpillar thinks it can

decide which way
it wants to go – to fly

or die. Should it take
an oath and dream

of having the loveliness
of the tiger butterfly or maybe

become a *friar* butterfly?
Caterpillar is a dreamer,

and a natural schemer.
In this changing light

the cuticle-shaped
drops of fluid

glow and glow
like red nectar.

It changes itself
as it hangs there,

wedged tightly as though
bolted with metal springs.

It now throws off brighter light –
a light of silver-purple

outlined in gold –
with golden trimmings.

1994

THE APPLE-MAGGOT FLY

In a Hudson Valley
winter apple orchard,
beneath one apple tree
in a row of apple trees,
snug inside your egg,
inside a rotten apple
hidden beneath red leaves,
you lay abed breathing
your slow larval sleep,
dreaming red,
without reason,
dreaming delicious,
longing too for the lost *she*
of your own delirious body,
through the long cold season.

Then, as pretty or ugly
as you want to be,
you chew your way
out of your own lace skin,
beginning to dream *lover,*
mindless of the fall,
mindless
of your puparium
cover – doing your own
maggot dance.

Larva-headed, cocky
and relaxed, and clear-winged,
you tunnel now into
the living corpse of winter
earth. You proceed where winter
hits with the least amount
of breast-pounding snow,
under the tongue
of a good layer of earth.

And in spring,
(I'm informed)
you are transformed,
(if you survived
the wasps) into
a proud pupa, fit to sit
up, heavy and big
as you're going to get.

All to this end:
to wait quietly
on perhaps the same apple
tree till *she* sees you waiting
and decides you are the one,
the only one she wants
to catch her *ovi*.
On the lookout for birds,

and to let other
females know you are spoken
for, she leaves a trail
of her droppings
all around you so they will
know to whom you belong.

1994

THE GREAT HORNED OWL

He glides, descending
to the forest floor –

his round face
like an African

mask, carved out
of soft wood.

He sails down smoothly
(his face as wide

as his shoulders
with big ears

jutting straight up
like horns) – descending

to the forest floor
where a mouse

scurries along.
And the wingspan

of the great night bird
spreads, showing

his white plumage
in this, his pale phase,

as he snatches it

he sings and dances
in the half-light,

scattering dry leaves,
spreading again

those great wings.
On the takeoff

he fans his fluffy
black-and-white tail.

1996

248

THE JAKE FLOWER

With a happy heart,
while singing to himself,
and with skin scrubbed sweet,
and now slapped with sweet water,

Jake puts on his Jane outfit,
the works – from underwear out:
romantic silks, satins, his camisole set,
embroidery cut to a tee,
spaghetti shoulder-straps,
hemline fit to choke like smoke.
Puts on his blazing red silk dress
the one with delicate ruffles
around wrists and around
and down from neck
to the pleated bottom,
above-the-knee, where everybody
can see his graceful flow
as he walks that walk. ("I'm a mess, honey!")
A formal white silk scarf hung
loosely around his neck, and flowing.
Nothing machine washable here. And in heels
and all. All that makeup:
light creams and powders
not quite right

for his dark skin.
But here he comes, wearing
the works – regal earrings, visionary eyelashes,
celestial shadow, nails painted pink,
and – you knew this was coming –
a handcrafted heart,
a great swollen broken handcrafted heart,
carrying all the sadness of the world,
while saying to himself, "I want
a real man, a pollinator. I want a child."

And Jake goes out, strolls out,
dressed to kill, with his small
bony butt twirling, laughing at himself,
looking to get laid,
checking himself in showcase windows.

And do you know there is a fungus
that disguises itself
as a flower – pretty and open,
sugar-nectar emphatic,
to lure unsuspecting
flower-visiting flyers to itself
(dreaming windswept spores)
in order to get fertilized,
to get its own "pollen"
(such as it is) transferred

elsewhere, to propagate,
to continue, to be antistatic,
spreading fungi glory,
spreading fungal spores all over.

But when Jake comes back,
sidewalk-worn, two eyes crossed,
back from his dreamtime,
you realize his bigger-than-life sorrow,
as he crawls in bed, alone,
and with a finger to his head
he pulls the trigger and dreams
he's a butterfly, unfertilized, sad, tired.

And just a little amazed
to still be alive and to hear
his own heart still singing.

1996

NO TIME FOR SELF-PITY

Always
I'm the one slightly slighted, he said.
But there is no why.
Desire is one thing.
The fall of events another.
Take migrating birds, black inkspots against sky.
You navigate while I snap pictures.
Wrens go south, flapping,
light as leaf tissue.
No self-pity, they just go,
giving up their nests,
with rose-pink bitterroot hanging down –
　　　go, go, go –
like the girl said that time in Italy,
　　　go, go go –
and if you could eat, say,
cherries in midair or eat spiders,
dig up earthworms and shit
from a telephone pole,
you too would have no time
for self-pity, no time
to ask yourself why
you get the cold shoulder.
You'd just go,

pecking at tree bark when you could,
eating a lot of stuff that looks back at you.
To avoid death, you'd go
in cold weather to stay warm,
stopping, say, in some ash tree
to catch your breath.
Then go on,
doing what comes naturally
on a long-distance flight.

1996

SEPTEMBER MENDOCINO

What do you hear up here?
    Same Shasta air, same Nevada air,
    same Sierra Nevada air, same rainsong air
    that lured Wait Whitman when he heard it.

But it is easier
    to find what is left of Walt Whitman
    these days, not in the sand, but
    in a musty bookshop
    over in Fort Bragg, where you sit,
    rather than seeing him
    walking a logging road,
    beating the underbrush with his long stick.

Now the question is:
    How good are the muffins in the morning fresh?
    They taste crunchy, still warm from the oven.
    Would Whitman eat one, you think?
    He would, he would, but he'd smell it first.

Can you smell the misty lands of the western shore?
    Yes, but not like a big net full of fresh fish.
    Not like that. You smell fresh pine in the wind.
    And back on the hidden road
    you really smell pine and redwood

as if they were still split open like watermelons
in the grass. Which grass? And back there,
on the track of a winding logging road,
giant log-trucks shooting by the turnoff
where we bought the dulcimer
at Mick's from Deb,
these trees whisper all day and certainly at night.

Can you come here without going to Russian Gulch
        or to Primitive Horse Camp, the Headlands?
        Skipping these, would you go away
        with less than a tourist should?

Do we any longer see what is befitting
        in these mountains?
        No bark a foot thick here.
        No. This is 1993, tree for tree.
        How many of the giant spirits
        of 1874 still stand as I wash
        my hands in the California coastal water?

So, is it necessary to still sing a California song?
        The song has nothing to do with whether or not
        this year is like Walt's year. It has to do with air,
        this air, this new air, fresh still in all essential ways,
        and singing through the redwoods' cold nights.

What else, then, do you hear?

       We hear dulcimer strings –

       that out-of-this-world sound. Nothing like it.

       And other things we heard?

       We heard about Jim's freshly baked muffins.

       Heard about the cottage out back,

       heard about the tree view,

       heard about water towers one and two.

       We heard about the pine furniture.

       And we heard about complete privacy.

       And friendly strangers around a breakfast table.

       A fire in the fireplace after dinner.

       We heard people up late downstairs

       talking with great excitement.

       We heard old Walt's wood spirits

       talking all through the night.

What do you see through the tree?

       Same giant redwood stand, back farther

       than we can beat our way to by land;

       same cold night corner-of-Pacific

       from our bed-and-breakfast window

       in old Joshua Grindle's house on the hill.

       Through the redwood branches,

       we saw Walt's spirit swimming

       out in the Pacific with its boots on,

       but still being clear

256

about "your average spiritual man,"
and clear about the "voice
of a mighty, dying tree
in the redwood forest dense."

But it's not the same there, anymore, Walt:
Not in Jackson State Forest,
not in Damme State Park,
not in Pigmy Forest.

What do you see when you stand
       out on Little Lake Road
       and gaze at Grindle's house?
You see the big white frame house
with wraparound ten-pillow porch,
you see your upstairs window.

What do you hear from here?
       We hear other tourists at breakfast
       talking about where they came from,
       talking about how long it's been
       since they were last here,
       back when the place was owned
       by somebody else, not by Jim
       and his wife. But we do not hear
       the crack! crack! crack!
       of the chopper's ax Walt heard.
       They're farther back.

How deep is the river – is it as deep as it was?
      It's deeper than the gift shops are high.
      That's for sure. Deeper than
      Rainsong Shoes or Paper Pleasures,
      Deeper than Papa Bear's Chocolate Haus
      or The Melting Pot and Papa Bird's put together.
      But really, how far down is that river?

Is this small cluster of shacks the remains
      of the big camp shanties of the 1870s?
      Pretty to think them
      the ones Walt wrote about, crowded together
      boastfully strung along the coast.
      Do you smell them, do they stink?
      Do they smell of fish?
      Fishermen think fish smell pretty good.
      What is their "unseen moral essence,"
      compared to, say, the trendy gift shops
      and their objectives?

So, what is coming up the mountain road for?
      For the romance of the wood spirits, still.
      And for our own romance in our oceanview room
      with its tiny sailboat wallpaper,
      ship's table and framed pictures of paddleboats.

And when we go away from here,
> what do we want to remember?
> What will we necessarily remember?
> What we heard in the air.
> What we smelled on the air.
> The smell of the fresh corn muffins.
> Just the things a tourist needs.

1995

DESCENDANT OF SOLOMON AND THE QUEEN OF SHEBA

Yellow flowers, yellow flowers.
Skim milk, honeybees and skim milk.
Smell of ponderosa leaves.
None of these images slap
their way into your sleep.

There: brown heads busted open
in an ocean of sunlight.
Sailing around in a lazy circle,
bloated blackflies
are sucked to stink
of decaying flesh.
This and every night in your sleep, this image,
over and over,
as you wake to dying, bloody dying,
seeing archangels weeping and
stepping from your ancient triptych,
tripping over bodies beside
the collapsed wall of your ruined basilica.
And your murals and memory too are ruined.
In your nightmare, where else is there to go
this morning – through which door?
I see you squatting under flying bullets
and plunging bayonets.

Bloated blackflies and you half-remember
what you were told: everyone is promised more.
Yellow flowers, smell of yellow flowers –
in the midst of spring garbage.

You, a brown man, full of trust,
shaking in the shade,
patient in the long shadows of Zagwa kings.
Do you find humility as you sweep the leaves?
You sweep pine needles under trees
in this my strange land.
What else is there to do here
but sweep up somebody's dust?
And maybe know the taste of mint,
crinkle of money, sound of larks.

But here even, a brown man like you,
from your homeland, in fact,
just shot through the head
this morning jogging with
a white woman in the park
across the street from his apartment.
Can you make sense of this craziness?

In your dark room, you're lucky
to wake from the gray nightmare
of starvation, lucky still to

possess power of taste, power of touch.
And so am I.
Lucky you to know what you know.
Over in your homeland
your ancient manuscript,
illuminated with colors still true,
manuscript of the fourth century
(before the birth of Christ) –
on a Judaic altar
(according to your sister) –
has not yet been pissed on
nor shot full of holes.
And your mother hasn't been strung up
with a rope and your sister is still a virgin.

See, a brown man like you,
framed like a pope in a doorframe
of display-light, understands better than we
how there is no sure plan
that anybody can surely depend on.
And I shake your brown hand
with my own and
the ocean is smaller.

1994

WAITER IN A CALIFORNIA VIETNAMESE RESTAURANT

With the smell of firebombing
still in his nose,
he brings our plates to the table
pausing for a vertiginous instant,
holding them as though they are two stones.
When he tries to smile his face
      turns purple like sky above
that Red River delta.
He once stood against a tree
with both arms above his head,
like somebody about to dance
flamenco, but he wasn't, it was
the time of the Spring Offensive,
and he was looking into the barrel
of a rifle held by a boy
whose trigger finger
      had turned to stone.

1989

BRIEF VISIT TO VENICE

From the train window
coming here, I saw the Autostrada
stretching alongside tracks,
cars racing us, saw the names,
hip to all the games on signs –
Montellago, Scorze, Piombino.
In the countryside cracked my side
at the sign on a farmhouse –
said Spend Summer Here, pale pink,
paler green. Lean and mean boys
hawking at the train speeding
toward Venice. In Venice
we push our way toward St. Mark's
caught up in the remarks
and shuffle of tourists,
hip to nothing
but the red scarf
leading them. Good
at crossing bridges,
skipping steps, we were out of step.
Called for help and got none.
Nuns in rows in the square.
Are they square, anywhere?
We played each other nights
like stringed instruments,

through the narrow streets,
walking in front of our own
long shadows, bright even at dusk.

1995–1998

NO SINGLE THING BY ITSELF

She carried a heavy load, but
her life was not a story.
It had no center.

Everything in it mattered.
Things alone and things together.
Her own smell.
In time, the right husband
at the right time.
A wedding ring
on the left-hand finger.
Her dead father's memory
swimming like goldfish
in her milky sleep.
Everything counted.
The red truck across the street.
Her unworn red dress.
Sad, lonely people
with acerbic wit.
Mean and nice servants.
First sentences.
Plotless dinner parties.
The great space called Life.
September in Spain.
Secrets – "I would die

if anyone reads these words."
Windows looking out
from dark rooms.
Taste, smell, touch, thought.
She counted everything.
She counted on things
being in their places.
Believed in everything –
the journey of sperm cells
swimming for survival
inside other women.
Fit, she accepted herself.
Survival of the fittest.
Believed in her dreams.
Though there was no
center to anything,
everything counted.
The cost of underwear.
The sound of trees.
The color of underwear.
What she wore.
Her student fees.
The right nursing home
for her dying mother.
Her mother's smell.
Her mother's swollen ankles.
Everything. All of it.

The hungry in India.
The told and the untold.
Untold millions dying.
The dying in Africa.
The dying in America,
dying without design.
Without line, or reason,
it all added up, counted,
meant something somehow.
Yet, in detail after detail,
while she carried
the weight of her life,
the pieces refused
to fit together.

1996–1998

CLAY BISON IN A CAVE

Clay-tan, eyeless,
voiceless, even in a sense weightless,
in motion yet motionless still
for centuries and centuries,
stuck in this motion
of climbing, perhaps lost, these
two Paleolithic bison,
heads lifted, strained back
to the black endless sky,
as they climb toward sunny grass.
Which black sky? Which grass?
Rock-step by rock-step,
up they go, on up and up.
The black sky at the top of the cave.
The grass that is always
more a promise in a dream
than that sweet kiss
blown by watercolored wind.

1996

STILLNESS AND VERTIGO

I enter.
What is that chanting?
Here
among vestments
and melons
bowls and brine kegs
filled
and crossbars of silver,
gilded bronze, velvet –
where dancing is done
in trick mirrors
where one's self
runs the risk of being lost
in the fibrous tissues
and fantasies of another,
you enter.
My entrance meets
yours on the turning floor.
We touch in the mirror,
crazed with fear
of the loss of balance,
like two sacrificial victims
waiting to be beheaded
and left to dry

in ceremonial sunlight,
as a concoction,
like wormwood.

1997

VIEW FROM HIS ROOM

His room was big and clean
and the scene from the window
was cheap and stayed still
long enough to be photographed
correctly. Always one to check
out the view from the window,
to see what was framed away.
All the same to stand still and look out
upon this place that could be home.
This place might be home someday,
seeing shutters flanked by rows
     of fenced backyards,
seeing a mother waving to him,
seeing a red garter belt hung
     on a clothesline,
seeing a pair of green stockings,
seeing a pink slip dancing in the wind.
And remembering
The Reverend Monsignor
     passing by
in his special car. These people
in some way may become his –
     uneasily his. The clothesline too,
a simple clothesline. What a miracle
     of thinness sloping through

the yard like a border
        between two countries,
a border between two yards,
a border between two
persons side by side.

1997–1998

AT THE ZOO IN SPAIN

Bound to the earth,
the pink flamingos
stand long
on one leg
in the shallow pool,
making not a sound.
With eyes closed,
they are meditating on
and dreaming of
their own rebirth.

1997

274

ARRIVING UNINVITED

Without the red splashed through the yellow,
in this ancient holy city, like an oil spill in the river,
the gray of the praying buildings would have
no purpose. The gold-yellow itself is not
a divine cluster of leaves. They are blessed
and scattered across some private
walled-in postage stamp of holy ground
of grass, alas, and no it's more than that.
You don't walk on this hallowed ground.
You don't pray on it.
This is the bed of the sea where you see
silver one minute and gold the next –
church colors gold and silver, any way
you look at them. The fine network of summer
is ending. The snow-blue sky now
this moment is holier than this city.
We are here but we remain as unknown
to this city as its lovers' true motives,
as unknowable as each pirate
or deposed monarch
wearing a blessed monocle,
strutting the narrow streets.
Arriving uninvited is risky.

1997

SANTA MARIA DEI FRARI

You are late for your train.
You linger anyway.
You know a Titian is there.
You looked, Madonna of the Pesaro Family.
You touched St. Peter and his great book.
You behold Madonna on her throne
formally receiving a kneeling
high military official: St. George and his soldiers.
The glitter of the swords catches your eye.
The Turkish prisoner is not happy.
Do you know the young woman
with big bright eyes? A member
of the Pesaro family. Half-hidden
by the figure of St. Francis,
bluntly in the foreground
you watch her gaze
around the saint out directly at you,
making you self-conscious. Leaving
Frari, you wander back
across Venice. You take a boat
over to St. George's. Inside,
Tintoretto's *Last Supper.*
You – an uninvited guest –
grab its energy
as it races away in the distance

like a night train
you yourself are already on,
coming straight back
into yourself.

1997

BIRDS

It's a summertime night
with hazel branches
drunk with yellow.
With the window open,
he's in bed after washing
his hands to hold
the precious book.
He closes his eyes
dreaming of migrating birds,
specks on the sky.
The room is charcoal gray.
Nice background
for his copper hands.
On the page the bird lands
on a fragile branch,
wings vibrate.
She's in bed too watching
him turning pages.
She shivers like a bird.
They're in their larval states,
suspended in animation.
After all
they are just-married.
Still mysterious to each other.
Now she throws the blue quilt back

exposing
his bright red underwings,
his nature. She too flashes
bright red under her wings.
The branch gives
beneath the bird's weight
as it touches down.
They seem among
late-blooming flowers.
Both watch for bats, spats, flaws.
This may be their life
of embracing
every other minute
while nesting deep
as in the crevice of a rock.
They sleep where no moth
will hibernate. *Birds know*
which branches will hold
their weight. As she
watches him read
she's drawn toward her own
wish, which is to rise
up and fly out of bed,
flapping her wings quietly,
until she is far away,
on her own, which is to say,
beyond the mystery

that surrounds the bedroom
and the bed where they sit.
As he turns the pages,
she counts each bird
that takes off from them,
dripping ink, as they go
out the window
into the summer night.

1995–1998

DARWIN'S DREAM

Unseen at forest edge
in morning light,
Darwin watches the parade
of little animals marching
up out of sea
waters so green,
and he's pleased
by sight
of their lunar rhythm.

Darwin says look,
the little beasts
with their lovely moony eyes
parading up from sea-womb.

Watching them scatter,
Darwin counts them going
south and east, west and north,
ranks breaking, rhythm shattered,
as they trot off in new rhythm,

into dark forest after dark forest
following scent of sea
in each leaf of each tree.

1998

HEARTLAND MUSIC

Crickets cranking shifting gears,
and I lie down
on creeping lily turf
beneath weeping branches,
sad and happy, listening
to the thumping rhythm
of my own heartbeat,
as if counting my last few minutes,
a rhythm I see repeated
in the pinkish red sky
covering me like glasswork.
I wish you were here.

Patchwork clouds
cast down occasional shadows,
now bumping along
the shallow gulf here, keeping rhythm
to the drum in my chest
full of wind chimes.
        Wish you were here.

Closing my eyes,
I listen to the tiny fingers
of wind plucking
and washing the wheat

in the field behind the house
where clusters of white flowers
spread wild, lingering
all around wheat like cattle
                ready to graze.

And rattling
my chimes too, it moves off,
pushing those clouds, the way
your backup chorus gets behind
your beating heart
when you are the solo.

1997–1998

ON THE NATURE OF PERSPECTIVE

Sometimes there is a point
without a point of view.

A train goes by nearby.
Its shadow rumbles along beside it.

Those geese are just dots
on the sky flying to Greece they say.

The clusters of Catima are Caterina
de' Medici's fingers dipped in grape.

You let them sprinkle their play
with their overlay of purple-blue.

I relax and glean the blossoms, because
I know of time chance makes a fool.

And this is the turning around
in the nick of time that catches

both the soft light and these things
off balance yet just right.

1997–1998

284

DOWNWIND

Odor of death everywhere.

You're on a ship
and they're serving you rotten meat,
maggots crawling in it.

Which reminds me of the Stanislavsky film
set in Russia where the mates
take over and cut the captain and his men

into little pieces and drop them
in the ocean of Albert Ryder's bad eyesight –

a view unexpected.

1963–1998

LOOKING AT IMAGES REFLECTED IN
THE SHOWCASE PLATE GLASS

Ours is the country of Jack Armstrong.
Long buildings exploding, earthquakes, floods.
Mass murderer lining up teenagers.
Heather says all she needs is a post office
and a liquor store – one liquor store, one post office.
I'm stuck in the city in a long dark subway tunnel.
She sneers driving for hours across blacktop,
with giant breasts winking at her from billboards.
I say look on the bright side, it's not all shallow or grim.
We got Smurf and Cabbage Patch, Nintendo and Pac-Man.
And we've found a way to dance to the slow heartache music
Trudy the waitress keeps punching
all day at the drive-in burger joint.
True, we could ask for more
but hey! around here we count our blessings.

1998

THE PERFECT MATCH

She's in a Gypsy skirt.
I'm in the decline of life.
I drag Achilles by the foot.
She's making copper deals.
I'm dealing in shipwrecks.
She rides a Monet racehorce.
I ride a da Vinci cackling hag.
She's unsurpassable.
I'm passing by in the wink of an eye.
I put up with the artificial melody of traffic.
She makes traffic stop
with her Carmen Miranda smile.
We are fauve figures light
as a bebop note – made
for each other on the run.
I dance her water lilies till I stop.
She sings my peonies till night.

1998

HAZY DAY IN THE COMPOSITION

Trying for a tigerish kind.
Something like a horse.
Keep this in mind – then blue.
The liquid world of geometry.
A lost-wax process.
Blue-mercurial.
Count the trees: four kinds.
Beach and sand then sky.
A dark alcove but less of it.
A column emerges briefly.
Yellow again then the sound.
All types then the sound again.
Pink baby in a white sack.
Bullfrog with green stripes.
As though it were a ghost town.

1998

DRAWING FROM LIFE

I wake to sounds
of garbage collectors
banging cans,
making their rounds,
wake to taxi horns.
I wake to a dragon slain by Cadmus.
Must I wake – ?
Must I stand tall?
To be both real
and drawn – that is reason
to stay, to endure the noise.
The window of this small room.
Poised in the room, I look out.
I see the rows and rows of wheat,
I see the pale green death-figure
whacking wheat left and left.
I see the death's-head moth,
floating around the booming
birth of Bacchus. Noise!
Everything today is water-
marked on Ingres paper.
I leave my dungeon
shirtless, shoeless, and wander
– by accident –
into Geronimo's cage

at the first World's Fair,
sit down with Geronimo –
endure the giggles,
endure the spitballs,
endure the peanuts,
endure the pennies,
the rotten apples.
Standing behind us
a grand old gorilla
lifts his unruly eyebrows,
wondering
what in hell
is he talking about.
Am I talking?
He strokes my clean
high cheekbones,
kisses my jawline.

1998

HARPS

In the yellow church he saw himself.
The sound spreads like bluebells.
A full figure with limestone skin.
An oxeye daisy smile.
She floats downstream in a canoe.
They can be lovers floating above wilderness.
Tasting timberline air.
They are in touching distance.
Surrounded by dancing angels.
She already knows her lines.
DNA in dialogue with RNA.
Light blue the garden back of the rectory.
Here, figures redesign themselves as shrubbery.
Tongues wag at miracles.
This is a miracle.
A relationship,
like a tree, she says, has growth rings.

1998

THREE VIEWS OF HORSE

after Susan Rothenberg

Side view
without saddle or eyeflaps,
head hanging, eyes closed.
Horse aches at forelock,
in fetlocks, in thighs,
in chest muscles.

Horse is action,
captured spirit,
even while motionless.

See this front view.
Horseflies circling.
Horse's ear twitching, tail flapping.

Now three-quarter view.
His chest out,
sheath hanging.
Fancy parade-stepping.

Arrested energy.

1996–1998

292

THE TEXTURES OF SPACE

I caught a jaybird in midflight.
I handed it to the cantor
singing his sorrow song.
He kissed it and set it free
to the delta, watching it fly up;
and I too watched the jay
narrow and dance the light,
seeing it now fly down
missing tree after tree,
then up again like the rhythm
of a sad song. And it flew finally
into open sky of brain tissue,
becoming just a dot
like the beginning of a disease
on the dense surface of the brain.

1998

THE DISPUTE

The garden is dark green and the king
has set up his kingdom here
for the afternoon. Waiting for the next case,
he sits on his throne of stone. Clouds move
in circles above. Red berries hang from
the overhead profusion of foliage.
The king is cornerstone and supreme shadow here.
But is that a winter sky
or just a chain saw working at the sun?

Now two women are escorted in.
The bailiff's face is a woodpecker's.
The woman in red carries a baby.
The one in green carries grief.
Her clubfoot has gone to sleep.
The king lifts his snow-covered head
like he's just been handed a prison sentence
and as he listens to the dispute laid out
he finally raises his hands and says,
"I've heard enough – we'll cut the baby in half!"
And when a scream spirals through the garden
it's not clear which woman has screamed –
then it's clear to the king because
the woman in green is weeping.

Beneath the poised sword the infant's
toes and fingers curve and twinkle.
And held against the tapestry of the sky
the bailiff's sword continues to glitter
from the light striking it like water against rock.

1998

MEASURE

Okay, today I'm the teacher.
This is related to all energy.
Watch the horse's eye flutter
just above the buckle
on the headstall. See, it is
an attempt to resolve the conflict
out of which all beauty
and glory come flying like birds.
Everything comes down
to the inexact position
from which things are measured.
Peck and pint.
Day and decade.
The curbing and the explosion.
Center and edge.
Flux vortex reflex solar cycle.
A train on a track running late.
Think of maps and miles,
think of gravity.
Even crutches propped under
performers after war
to keep them from falling out
of their own exhausted bodies
are first measured to fit.
Gravity can be measured precisely.

Think of a nun in the prayer position.
She is in conflict with gravity.
Conflict can be measured precisely.
This is as close as we can get.
And this is as close as we need to be.

1998

AGING TOGETHER

– for P.

I watch myself aging in your eyes.

My heart in my chest sits high on stilts
and leans forward for the sunlight
that comes down through my ribs
at midmorning. It is still a hopeful heart.

My face still has two sides.
And my hands each have a pocket to sleep in.
Just like yours.

You stand near an old stone doorway,
shading your eyes from the sun.
The church bells are ringing again.
Each ding or dong has its own personality.

Across the way two women stand at a gate
feeding pigs. The pigs grunt and grind, watching us.

All night the majestic church bells ring,
setting a rhythm for our sleep as you sleep
peacefully beside me and I beside you.

In the morning we climb all the way
to the top of the hill for a panoramic view.
We see our village below by the bay.

The eagle with feet full of the possibility of stars
makes so much possible for us,
but it is our own love for each other
that makes the difference.

We are growing older gracefully together.
We've taken to aging like a dog to its collar.

1998

THE SLAVE TRADE:
VIEW FROM THE MIDDLE PASSAGE

I

I am Mfu, not a bit romantic, a water spirit,
a voice from deep in the Atlantic:
Mfu jumped ship, made his escape, to find relief
      from his grief on the way,
long ago, to Brazil or Georgia or Carolina –
      he doesn't know which;
      but this is real, not a sentimental
landscape
      where he sleeps free in the deep waves,
        free to speak his music:
      Mfu looks generously in all directions
        for understanding of the white men
          who came to the shores
            of his nation.

Mfu looks for a festive reason,
something
      that might have slipped.

Mfu looks back at his Africa,
      and there at Europe,
      and over there at the Americas,

where many of his kin were shipped
and perished, though many survived.
                    But how?
In a struggle of social muck. Escape?
                            No such luck then or now.

And Mfu hears all around him a whirlwind
        of praise, explanation, insinuation,
doubt, expression of clout –
        "It was a good time to be white,
        British, and Christian" (H.A.C. Cairns).
And remembering the greed of the greedy white
        men of Europe, greed for –
ivory, gold, land, fur, skin, chocolate, cocoa,
tobacco, palm oil, coffee, coconuts, sugar, silk,
Africans, mulatto sex, "exotic" battles,
        and "divinely ordained slavery."

And it was, indeed, with reverie,
        heaven on earth for white men.

But Mfu is even more puzzled by the action
        of his own village:
Mfu, a strong young man, sold in half-light,
        sold in the cover of night and muzzled
        (not a mistake, not a blunder);
        sold without ceremony or one tap

of the drum,
    sold in the wake of plunder –
            for a brush not a sum of money
            but a mere shaving brush,
            sold without consent of air fish water
                    bird or antelope,
            sold and tied with a rope and chain
            (linked to another young man
            from Mozambique's coast,
            who'd run like a streak
            but ended anyway in a slave boat
            without a leak or life preservers);
sold to that filthy Captain Snelgrave,
sold by his own chief, Chief Aidoo.
Sold for a damned shaving brush.
        (And Chief Aidoo, who'd already lived
                sixty winters,
        never had even one strand of facial hair.)
Sold for a shaving brush.
        Why not something useful?
        Even a kola nut? A dozen kola nuts?
                Six dozen kola nuts?
Sold for a stupid shaving brush.
        And why didn't the villagers object?
        (After all, he'd not been sold from jail,
        like Kofi and Ayi and Kojo and Kwesi
        and that girl-man Efua.)

And now Mfu's messenger, Seabreeze, speaks:
    "Chief Aidoo merely wanted your
        young wife but
    before he could get his hands on her,
    she, in grief, took her own life –
        threw herself in the sea."

Here in Mfu's watery bed
    of seaweed
he still feels the dead weight of Livingstone's
    cargo
on his head, as he crosses –
    one in a long line of strong black
        porters –
    the river into East Africa;

    in his seafloor bed of ocean weeds
    he still hears white men gathered in camp
    praising themselves in lamplight,
        sure of their mission –
    "Go ye therefore, and teach all
        nations,
    baptizing them…" (Matthew 28:19).

Mfu, raised from seed a good boy – to do all
    he could –
        never went raving mad at his father,

never shied from work, one
to never mope:
therefore when father said hold
the shaving mirror
for the white man, he held the shaving
mirror
for the white man, teaching himself
to read
the inscription: Kaloderma Shaving Soap.

But now Mfu, like a tree, is totally without
judgment
or ambition, suspended between
going and coming
in no need of even nutrition –
gray, eternal –
and therefore able to see, hear, and know
how to shape memory into a thing of wholeness
and to give this memory
not "the Negro revenged" voice
of abolitionist Wm. Cowper –
bless him –
but to see, say, what went into the making
of what, in those days, they called
Negrophobia.

II

To understand the contour,
Mfu must tour deep into Europe first,
            explore
its sense of Mother Nature: Mother Nature
        in Europe is a giant pink pig
        with a black baby at one tit
        (this is good Europe: charitable, kind,
                compassionate Europe)
        and a white baby at the other. A sucking
                sound,
            plenty to go around.

And in the background,
        without thought of remission, a band
        of white slave-catchers
                force Africans into submission
                (this is bad Europe: evil,
                    mercenary Europe)
                in order to chain them,
                hand to hand and leg to leg
                and ship them into slavery
                    in the new land.

Both Europes baffle Mfu.
Could it be solely about greed and profit?
But he must try to understand it,

first, the good Europe.
　　　He pictures this:
　　　In a longhouse somewhere
　　　　　on the coast
　　　of West Africa about fifty
　　　　　Africans,
　　　　in simple white cotton robes
　　　　are gathered in a dim light,
　　　　each awaiting his or her turn
　　　　to be dunked head-down
　　　　into a big wooden bucket
　　　　　of water.
Two rosy pink Christian white men,
　　　in slightly more elaborate white robes,
　　　in attendance – a link, surely, to heaven.
　　　　They do the dunking.
These are the good white men
　　　who wear Josiah Wedgwood's
　　　　medallion
　　　of a pious-looking African face
　　　with the inscription:
　　　"Am I not a man and a brother?" (1787).

But what is *really* happening?
　　　One culture is modifying another,
　　　and in the process (perhaps unwittingly)
　　　modifying itself, in the name of its god;

as a Liverpool slaver, with its wretched cargo,
    slides easily by
    headed for the West Indies
    or a port at Carolina,
    with bodies packed in the pit.

The good white monk on his knees in prayer,
    not interested in the gold of Afric
    or the Bugaboo or whether or not
        a European looks more
            like an orangutan
        than does, say, an Ethiopian.
(And besides, the orangutan is not an African
    animal.)
So, don't tell him stories
    of this man-of-the-forest
    kidnapping black babies,
thinking they his own kin.
Don't waste your time.
Don't tell him a good savage is one
    who will climb
    happily up a tree for you
and fetch you a piece of fruit like a good monkey.

Don't tell him your heathen jokes.
Don't laugh at Casper, at the birth of Christ.
Don't make fun of the Hottentots.

Don't try to convince him that Africans have
        no souls. Souls are not proven. Period.
The white monk, sin or not,
        has a secret vision of the Queen of Sheba,
        as a healing spirit for the downtrodden
                blacks,
and though this secular dream is out of rhyme
        with his devotion, much of his time is
                spent
on his vision of the Sable Venus,
        herself a Creole Hottentot,
        surrounded by chubby pink cherubs;
        he prays to black Saint Martin
        and to black Saint Maurice,
                in armor, patron saint
                of the Crusade
                against the Slavs,
the monk prays to the black Madonna,
who certainly must know something he doesn't
        know,
                        prays to all the white saints too
        (and you can name them)
and to Jesus, Mary, and Joseph.

The white monk prays that these lean Children
        of Ham
                        will be washed clean

by the spirit and say of the Lord –
                made as white
                            as the light of day;
made to sparkle the way the little Dutch children
                wanted to make
                their African playmate shine from
                and take to Snow-White Soap.

Anyway, at the very least,
                black souls could be made pure
                            as snow.
                No more niggling over that issue.
                Pure as snow, far from the mistletoe,
that thing too terrible to touch.
                And then when a French soldier
                brings home
                an African wife the village
                grief and fear
will surely fall to the ground like a leaf.

Mfu listens to the prayer
                and is puzzled by the contradiction
                implicit in its quest. It conceals a tyranny
                            surely
                                    not innate,
one Mfu would like to believe is not meant,
                or mean-spirited.

The implication, though, is unfortunate.
But Mfu remembers many such occasions
    when such good men prayed and took
        action too
            in the name of goodness-over-sin
            that led to no good for anybody:
    That out-of-breath five-year war
        in Suriname (1792).

They took and hung the leader
    on a hook by one of his ribs
    leaving him without a tear
    on the seashore to die
    a slow death.
The white monk, by the way, prays
    that the white Venus and the black
        eunuch,
    seen together like white on rice,
    will remain cool, nice, and chaste.
    The eunuch, after all, he knows
    is not Peter Noire. And even Peter Noire
    can be made to leap
        out of a box
like those that French children play with:
    where a black Martinican maid,
    complete with apron and headrag,
    springs up with a jolly smile,

ready to dust.
Or Black Peter could serve as Bamboulinette,
　　　where we use his mouth as an ashtray.

Mfu is not sad,
　　　but he now wonders
　　　how necessary is it to give examples
　　　of the deeds of *bad* white men
when there were so many jolly good sinless
　　　deeds
　　　　　of the exceptional men of pink skin.
We have so many who fought for the dignity
　　　of all human beings. (But then,
　　　is there not something in *all* men
　　　that must be resisted –
　　　especially by themselves?)
And Mfu also wonders at the noble, dignified
　　　presence
　　　　　of black intellectuals and military leaders
among the good Europeans:
There is Jean-Baptiste Belley, sad, ironic,
　　　sardonic,
　　　　　aging, elegant, in the French Army,
　　　　　a captain during the French Revolution,
fighting, no doubt, for justice for all,
　　　with strong memories
　　　of having been born a Senegalese slave

at remote Goree (1747). Surely
this man
lived with irony as if it were a cancerous
sore
in his throat.

III

Ah ha! Mfu can now see the Americas from here.

There is a group of Maroons being ambushed
by white overseers with guns
in moonlight in the bushes,
being yanked and gathered together
on the Dromilly Estate, Trelawny.

Haitian soldiers, crushing Napoléon,
placing ropes around the necks
of French soldiers and pulling them up
by way of pulleys to hang them
dangling from stakes,
to hang in the sun till they die.
And Hansel to Gretel:
"I'm afraid to go
to Africa because cannibals may
eat me
as they do one another."
Little Red Riding Hood to her

grandmother:
"Dig, what makes your mouth so big?"

And Ignatius Sandro, there,
      with that wonderful, whimsical
         gaze of his.
      No tears.

A crying Barbados mulatto girl on her knees
      before a planter.
His head thrown back, face drinking the sky,
      and with eyes closed, lace open,
his expression is both one of deep pleasure
      and great agony.

A Jamaican Creole noblelady sits on a porch
      while a black slave fans her.

Because of one slip,
a Sambo, white as his tormentors,
      strapped over a barrel,
        is being beaten with a bullwhip,
        and his entire backside is beet-red
          with blood.

A giant snake, sixty yards long,
      drops from a massive, ancient tree

onto the back of a black horseman,
    right or wrong, you see,
    and wraps itself around both,
            squeezing
till the horse and the man,
    taking all they can stand,
            stop moving, then swallows first
the man then the horse.

Mfu can also see farther north – Georgia and
    Carolina:
            Black men women and children bent
                working – out of breath –
                the cotton the corn the cane,
                from can't-see to can't-see,
                from birth till death,
                with no stake in their labor.

            Never will forget the day,
            Never will forget the day,
            Jesus washed my sins away.

Who is that pink-faced general, dying?
    lying on the ground dying out there,
as the Battle of Bunker Hill rages on?
Another general, one who will perhaps
    become president, fights his way

free of a cluster of redcoats,
          without feeling the slightest thrill
          while, on horseback
          in the background,
his slaves watch for him to botch it.

                    Pharaoh's army sunk in the sea,
                    Pharaoh's army sunk in the sea,
                    Sho am glad it ain't me.

And a Negro soldier (strong as a Wagogo
          warrior and
                    brave as KaMpande,
                              King of the Zulu)
          aims his rifle at a redcoat
          while a major points
the frailest pink finger
          ever in danger of being shot off
          in a revolutionary war.

                    Two white horses side by side,
                    Two white horses side by side,
                    Them the horses I'm gon ride.

A newspaper item: "And good white men
have come to believe that perhaps the sin
is not in keeping the niggers in chains but in releasing

them." ("Catch a nigger by the toe...?"
"Let my people go!")

A cartoon (1789):
> A black man dressed like an English gentleman
> is bludgeoning a poor, suffering white man over
> the head with an ignorant-stick. And in the
> background: Similar configurations dot the
> diminishing landscape. Message: Let them go
> and they will enslave you. Rationale: Abolition
> is folly.

This here is the white woman, France,
    (this time without the fabled black
        eunuch)
    with her arms outstretched to the slaves
    on knees before her,
        with arms lifted toward her
          thigh,
while Frossard watches with the light
    of an approving smile in his eye.

Jefferson strokes his chin,
thinking about freeing his slaves.
Here they come around the bend.
But he says oh well, maybe not.
Rise Sally rise. Wipe your weeping eyes.

Washington, on his deathbed, frees his slaves.
Thanks a lot.

> *On my way to heaven,*
> *Yes, Lord, on my way to heaven,*
> *On my way to heaven, anyway.*

Mfu remembers an Ashanti Juju girl
 (who gave him a coin)
 saying, "We must believe that the good
 in human beings will prevail."
  And on front of the coin:
  Nemesis, antique goddess
  with raised left arm.
  Right hand holds olive branch.
  Obverse:
  Face of a young African man,
  sensitive and intelligent.
  And the inscription:
  "Me miserum."
This relic, the best, the girl said, was given to her
 by a never-mean Danish traveler from
 the West Indies,
 where he'd seen, without reverie,
 the abolition of slavery
  in 1792.

Sister Mary wore three
links of chain,
Sister Mary wore three
links of chain,
Glory, glory to His name…

IV

Mfu says this is to strain against the insanity
      that welcomes us at the other end:
        Where one does not believe there is hope,
and one strains too to keep the gentle face
      of, say, Carl Bernhard Wadstrom,
          white man,
      bent over Peter Panah, black man,
teaching him to read.
And wish the configuration
    said something more
    than it does.

Mfu remembers Equiano.
    Equiano (1789) said: "We are almost a
    nation of dancers, musicians, and poets."
        And although we're more,
          much much more,
let's have a revival –

Why not celebrate?
If nothing else,
it can't hurt to celebrate survival.

1993–1994

ACKNOWLEDGMENTS

The selections from *Swallow the Lake,* published by Wesleyan University Press, 1970, are reprinted by permission of Clarence Major;

Selections from *Private Line,* published by Paul Breman, Ltd., 1971, London, are reprinted by permission of Clarence Major;

Selections from *Symptoms and Madness,* published by Corinth Press, 1971, are reprinted by permission of Clarence Major;

Selections from *The Cotton Club,* published by Broadside Press, 1972, are reprinted by permission of Clarence Major;

Selections from *The Syncopated Cakewalk,* published by Barlenmir House, 1974, are reprinted by permission of Clarence Major;

Selections from *Inside Diameter: The France Poems,* published by Permanent Press, 1985, are reprinted by permission of Clarence Major;

Selections from *Surfaces and Masks,* published by Coffee House Press, 1988, are reprinted by permission of Coffee House Press and Clarence Major;

Selections from *Some Observations of a Stranger at Zuni in the Latter Part of the Century,* published by Sun and Moon Press, 1989, are reprinted by permission of Sun and Moon Press and Clarence Major.

All poems listed below are previously uncollected. They are reprinted by permission of Clarence Major, and originally appeared as follows:

el carno emplumado 28 (October 1968): "Saving Just the Real";

CAPS: Poems by CAPS Fellows, 1970–1975 (1976): "First," "Sand Flesh and Sky";

Aspen Anthology (Fall 1978): "Pencil Sketch";

New Departures 14 (1982): "Riders";

Callaloo: A Journal of African-American Arts and Letters 20, Vol. 7, No. 1 (1984): "Posing," "Round Midnight";

Callaloo: A Journal of African-American Arts and Letters 21, Vol. 7, No. 2 (Spring/Summer 1984): "Study for a Geographical Trail";

The Literary Review, Vol. 25, No. 4 (Summer 1982): "The Other Side of the Wall," "Bernardston";

Black American Literature Forum, Vol. 23, No. 3 (Fall 1989): "The Swine Who's Eclipsed Me";

John O'Hara Journal, Vol. 5, Nos. 1 & 2 (Winter 1982): "Love against Death";

Words on the Page, The World in Your Hands: Book One, edited by C. Lipkin and V. Solotaroff, Harper & Row, 1990: "Apple Core";

The Kenyon Review, Vol. XIII (Fall 1991): "Train Stop";

The Jazz Poetry Anthology, edited by S. Feinstein and Y. Komunyakaa, Indiana University Press (1991): "Un Poco Loco";

Brilliant Corners: A Journal of Jazz and Literature, Vol. 1, No. 1 (1996): "In Walked Bud with a Palette";

Callaloo: A Journal of African-American Arts and Letters, Vol. 13, No. 2 (1990): "Being and Becoming," "The String" (as "Cat Mother"), "Unwanted Memory"; "Dance Floor";

Gathering of The Tribes 6 (Winter/Spring 1995/96): "Bricks and Sleep";

African-American Review, Volume 28, No. 1 (Spring 1994); "Frenzy" (as "On Trying to Imagine the Kiwi Pregnant); "Wyoming"; "A Slow Process" (as "On Watching a Caterpillar Become a Butterfly"); "The Apple-Maggot Fly" (as "I Was Looking for The University"); "The Slave Trade: View from The Middle Passage";

Michigan Quarterly Review, Vol. XXXI, No. 2 (Spring 1992): "Honey Dripper";

Callaloo: A Journal of African-American Arts and Letters, Vol. 19, No. 2 (1996): "The Great Horned Owl," "Clay Bison in a Cave";

Urbanus Magazine (Summer 1996): "No Time for Self-Pity";

New American Writing 13 (Fall/Winter 1995): "September Mendocino";

New Letters: A Magazine of Writing and Art, Vol. 60, No. 4 (1994): "Descendant of Solomon and the Queen of Sheba";

From Both Sides Now: The Vietnam War and Its Aftermath in Poetry, edited by P. Mahony, New York: Scribner (1989): "Waiter in a California Vietnamese Restaurant";

Witness, Vol. 11, No. 2 (1997): "Arriving Uninvited."

ABOUT THE AUTHOR

In 1970 Clarence Major's first collection, *Swallow the Lake,* won the National Council on the Arts Award and a year later his poetry was honored with a New York Cultural Foundation prize. Widely published in such periodicals as *Kenyon Review, The Michigan Quarterly Review, Literary Review,* and *The American Poetry Review,* Major has also been represented in leading anthologies such as *Postmodern Poetry in America 1950 to the Present – A Norton Anthology* (1994) and many others. Author of nine previous volumes of poetry, Major has read his poetry at the Guggenheim Museum, the Library of Congress's Folger Theater, in hundreds of universities, theaters, and cultural centers in the United States, as well as in England, France, Germany, Italy, Ghana, and Yugoslavia. In Yugoslavia he represented the United States at the International Poetry Festival. He is also the editor of two poetry anthologies widely used in university classes, and several books of fiction, including *Dirty Bird Blues.* Clarence Major lives in Davis, California.

BOTH THE TEXT AND TITLE faces were designed for digital composition by Matthew Carter. Galliard, the text face, reflects the spirit of type cut by Robert Granjon in the late 1500s, while Mantinia, used in the titles, is based on letterforms found in the fifteenth century paintings of Andrea Mantegna. Both faces have Renaissance energy and confidence. Interior design and composition by Valerie Brewster, Scribe Typography. Cover image *Configurations,* by Clarence Major, acrylic, 30″ × 40″, 1978–1991. Printed on archival quality Glatfelter Author's Text (acid-free, 85% recycled, 10% post-consumer stock) at McNaughton & Gunn.